UNIX™
Shell Programming

UNIX™
SHELL PROGRAMMING

Lowell Jay Arthur

A Wiley-Interscience Publication

JOHN WILEY & SONS

New York / **Chichester** / **Brisbane** / **Toronto** / **Singapore**

Library of Congress Cataloging in Publication Data:

Arthur, Lowell Jay, 1951–
  UNIX shell programming.

  On t.p. the registered trademark symbol "TM" is
superscript following "UNIX" in the title.
  "A Wiley-Interscience publication."
  Includes index.
  1. UNIX (Computer operating system) 2. UNIX Shells
(Computer programs) I. Title.

QA76.76.O63A77   1985   005.4'3   85-22623
ISBN 0-471-84932-4
ISBN 0-471-83900-0 (pbk)

Printed in the United States of America

0 9 8 7 6 5 4

To Alice Hargrove

Preface

In the summer of 1975, I was a lowly IBM batch COBOL programmer. Who would have imagined that I would soon be thrust into Bell Labs— the fiercest nest of UNIX zealots I have ever seen? Brian Kernighan, one of the "fathers" of UNIX, is reported to have said the following about IBM COBOL programmers: "Watching an IBM programmer do anything is like watching a man kick a whale across the beach with his bare feet." This is only hearsay (or *heresy* as an IBMer might perceive it), but in the UNIX world such enormous problems rarely occur. The man would have spent his leisure hours collecting shells on the beach.

Shells, UNIX command language programs, are the essence of the power and productivity of UNIX. They allow the UNIX programmer, word processor, manager, or whoever to perform vast amounts of work at a terminal. An experienced Shell user typically outperforms his or her peers.

A novice user will often look at Bourne or C Shells and come away discouraged. The Shells seem too complex . . . too new. But when fully understood, the Shell provides the power to manipulate documents, build programs, communicate with other users, and generally be more productive.

This book is not designed for the novice UNIX user; I would recommend reading any of the excellent introduction-to-UNIX books before tackling this one. Anyone with some experience, however, should find the material easy to read, with sufficient examples to get hooked on the

UNIX Shell. I wrote this book for people who want to get the most out of their UNIX system. Vanilla UNIX hardly provides major benefits to the user community. It is only through the use of the Shell to automate repetitive work that UNIX becomes a tool and not a burden. UNIX should be ballet . . . not hockey.

I organized this book to reflect how I think about UNIX and the use of the Shell. The first chapter describes the rise of UNIX as one of the major operating systems currently available. It also introduces the basic concepts of the Shell, some of which will seem radical to almost anyone, especially IBM-oriented users, even though the benefits have been touted in the *IBM Systems Journal* (Stevens, 1982).

Chapters 2–5 get into the heart of Shell programming: commands, control structures, interactive use of the Shell, and creating Shell programs. A novice Shell user should master the concepts presented in these chapters before continuing with more advanced topics.

Chapter 6 addresses UNIX implementations on microcomputers and variations on the Shell. UNIX was the first micro-based operating system to provide multitasking. Its dominance in the microcomputer world will continue to grow because of its portability and simplicity.

Because UNIX has gained a reputation as lacking "user friendliness," I have included a chapter on creating user friendly interfaces using Shell. Ergonomics are an increasingly important part of any computer system.

In Chapter 8, you will find tips on a variety of advanced Shell programming techniques: maintainability, reliability, efficiency, and handling interrupts. This chapter may contain more information than the casual Shell user needs, but every UNIX installation has a number of toolsmiths who build Shell programs for use by everyone. They are the prime audience for this chapter.

The remaining chapters discuss how the Shell can aid a variety of users with different interests. Some users only handle documents, others numbers, others graphics, and still others program in C language or send jobs to other machines. Each chapter will appeal to particular users; they are included for your convenience. The last chapter discusses the Shell environment and system administration.

This book is by no means a completely definitive text on the Shell. New Shell tools appear in each system release. UNIX user groups are constantly building and sharing tools. A good Shell user is always on the lookout for new tools to improve productivity. New commands may chew up more computer resources, but machines are cheaper than people. The same work could be done with a pen and paper, but kicking whales is neither fun nor productive. Let the UNIX Shell go to work for you.

As you can tell, in the years since the summer of 1975, I have become a UNIX zealot. Over ten years of working in alternating UNIX, Honeywell, and IBM environments has helped confirm my bias. I hope that this book will help start you in the same direction. If you are already a dedicated UNIX user, I hope that it will broaden your creative and productive horizons.

LOWELL JAY ARTHUR

Denver, Colorado
January 1986

Contents

UNIX™
Shell Programming

CHAPTER

1

Introduction
to the UNIX Shell

The UNIX Shell is the key to improving productivity and quality in a UNIX environment. The Shell can automate repetitive tasks, find where you left things, do things while you are at lunch or asleep, and perform a host of other timesaving activities. The use of the Shell can double, triple, or quadruple your productivity at the terminal. The Shell accomplishes these things by letting you create tools to automate many tasks. It enables you to construct prototypes of programs, procedures, or tools. The speed with which you can build a working prototype, enhance it to provide exactly what you need, or just throw it away and begin again, will allow you the flexibility to create exactly the right tool without a lot of coding, compiling, and testing. It will rarely be necessary to do things by hand, because the Shell can grapple with almost any problem. The Shell derives its power from UNIX.

1

1. WHAT IS UNIX?

UNIX is a time-sharing operating system. It was originally developed by Ken Thompson on a DEC PDP 7 because he wanted a more flexible environment for programming. Others with similar interests came to his aid, and soon UNIX became a reality. UNIX departed from most traditional approaches to operating systems in that it handled all input and output (I/O). UNIX simplified I/O by having all files and devices look the same to any command that used them. Files contain data as streams of characters—no records, no varying record sizes, and fewer problems. Because of this uniqueness, every program could be designed to accept input from any other program. Each program could perform a single unique function and be connected to other programs, devices, or files via the operating system. This simple design detail gives UNIX and the Shell much of their power.

Following the development of UNIX, many software developers contributed additional user-oriented tools. These tools were packaged as an extension to UNIX called the Programmer's Workbench (PWB). This has since been included into the standard package, UNIX. The original Shell was rewritten by S. R. Bourne about 1975, giving us the current version of the Shell known as the "Bourne Shell," which runs under AT&T's UNIX Version 2.0 through System V. Students and professors working at the Berkeley campus created another version of the Shell known as the "C Shell" that is useful for C language programmers. It runs under Berkeley UNIX, 4.2 BSD. Which of these Shells will dominate the market is yet to be seen, but AT&T's version 5.0 was the first attempt to standardize the UNIX system and the Shell. I expect to see both Shells provided in future releases of UNIX.

2. WHAT IS THE SHELL?

The Shell is almost exactly what it sounds like; it is a hard casing that provides a friendly environment to the user while protecting each user from every other one. It allows each user to do whatever he or she wants to do without affecting any of the other users. When a user logs into a UNIX system, the operating system automatically starts a unique copy of the Shell under which the user can perform any function available. It is this protected yet powerful environment that gives each user the ability to be more productive.

3. WHEN TO USE THE SHELL

Anytime you enter a UNIX command, you are using the Shell. To increase productivity, use the Shell whenever you are faced with doing a repetitive task to many files or whenever you must do the same task many times a year. It's as simple as that. People, by necessity, are forced into repetitive tasks: a group of documents are delayed and each of the dates must be changed; the originator changed jobs and the names in the document must be changed; a department name must be changed in 400 documents; reports must be produced every month with associated graphs and attachments; or the figures have changed and must be revised. Each of these tasks can be automated with a Shell program.

You should use the Shell interactively at your terminal to automate any task that you probably will not need again. There are many situations that occur daily that could benefit from use of the repetitive features of Shell, but they do not require the creation of a separate Shell command—these problems can be solved with interactive use of the Shell. More on interactive Shell usage in Chapter 3—Shell Control Structures.

You should not use the Shell when the task is too complex, requiring a larger machine and different tools: you wouldn't use a hammer to drive a spike into a railroad tie or a spade to dig an irrigation canal. Similarly, you wouldn't use a steam shovel to put in a flower bed. It is rarely productive to use the Shell when the task is not repetitive (e.g., changing "and" to "or" in a document, removing a single file). Instead, use the Shell to automate tasks done every day, week, or month. (If you only perform a task once a year, you will probably forget where you put the Shell and what it is called.) Also use the Shell to automate anything that requires text manipulation: selecting data, adding numbers, printing statistics, or whatever. Finding the right data in a mound of reports is simple for the Shell and cumbersome for people. Manipulating data and putting it into printable form is also tedious and unreliable. The Shell, as you will soon see, can do all of these things quickly and reliably.

4. PRODUCTIVITY AND THE SHELL

Studies (Thadhani, 1984) have shown that an average programmer may spend 20–25 hours a week at the terminal. Ninety-five percent of that time involves "human-intensive" activities like editing and data manipulation. As homes, offices, and businesses become increasingly automated, 20–25 hours may climb to 30–35. To make people more productive at the terminal, response times must be kept to a minimum (under 1 second) or people must be allowed to automate more of their human-intensive activities. The Shell and its tools have been designed and optimized to automate many of these activities. It requires some insight into the Shell and its usage to derive these benefits, but as you will see in the following chapters, it only takes a little ingenuity to become more productive.

Since the Shell can automate most of the recursive tasks, which encompass 50–80% of the human-intensive activities, it is little wonder that the Shell can double or triple productivity. The simplicity of UNIX files and the file system design makes this possible.

5. UNIX FILES

UNIX files are unique because they are basically free form. Each file is just a sequence of characters (Figure 1.1). Lines or records are delimited by the newline (nl) character. The end of a file is delimited by an end-of-file (EOF) or end-of-tape (EOT). Since every file can be read character by character and produce output the same way, every program available to the Shell has been designed to handle just this one simple file. The output from any program can be used as input to any other program. This design feature allowed the originators of UNIX to create simple, modular programs to perform single functions. Each function, although trivial when viewed as a single entity, becomes vastly more important when combined with other singular functions to do virtually any kind of text manipulation.

The UNIX Shell is the key to improving your productivity\n
and quality in a typical UNIX environment.\n The Shell can
automate repetitive tasks,\n find where you left things,\n do
things while you are at lunch,\n and a host of other time
saving activities.\n\0

Figure 1.1   A UNIX file.

UNIX files reside in a hierarchical file system or inverted tree, like
the one shown in Figure 1.2. To implement this structure, UNIX uses a
special file known as a directory. It has exactly the same form as any
other file except that it contains entries that point to the directory
above it and any files or directories below it. Each directory is a fork in
the tree, from which other branches may grow. This facility is useful
for organizing data. In the example, my user identification, lja, resides
under the file system /unix1. Under my ID, there are directories for
source code (src), shell commands (bin), and documents (doc). These
names are short because most people are terrible typists. Longer
names like sourcecode or documentation can rarely be typed without
error and typing them is time-consuming. Even my ID, lja, is nothing
but initials. Under src are directories for "C" language (c.d) and
COBOL (cobol.d). The ".d" suffix makes them readily identifiable as
directories. Under each of these directories are a variety of files. Just
by use of directories and their names, I can usually find what I need in
short order. Finding where you left something in a UNIX file system is
often a challenge, especially if you have 30–100 files in a directory.

Directories and data files are not the only types UNIX offers. There
are other special "files" that are not really files at all, but devices like
terminal handlers, disk drives, tape drives, and so on. These will be
discussed in detail in the advanced material. Any of these files can be
processed using a Shell command to filter or enhance the data.

6.   FILTERS

You should think of most Shell commands as filters like the one shown
in Figure 1.3. They have a single input, called standard input (ab-
breviated stdin), that gives them a character at a time. Each command

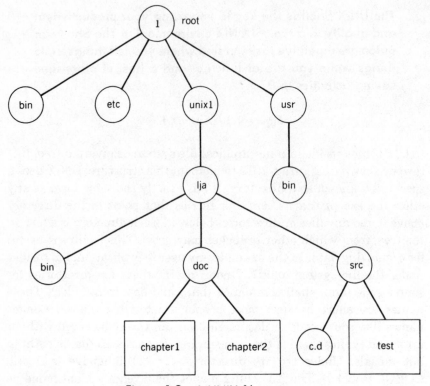

Figure 1.2 A UNIX file system.

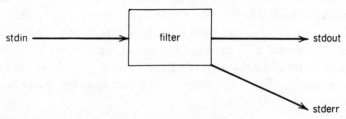

Figure 1.3 A Shell filter.

6

also has two outputs: standard output (stdout) and standard error (stderr). Each command filters data from the standard input or refines it in some fashion and passes it to the standard output. Any errors that it encounters are passed to stderr. Errors rarely occur, however, because most UNIX commands are designed to take intelligent default actions in most situations. If, for example, you don't assign a file as stdin, then the Shell assumes that the terminal is stdin. If you don't assign a file as standard output, then the Shell again assumes that the terminal is standard output. One of the dumbest things you will ever do is type a command such as *cat* (concatenate and print) followed by a return and then wonder what is happening:

cat<return>

What is happening? See Figure 1.4. The Shell is waiting for you to type input from the screen, and it will display it back to you when you are done. To get out of this command, you must hit the "break" or "delete" key, or type ctrl(d) for end-of-file.

The *cat* command is the simplest of the Shell's filters. It does not change the data; it takes the standard input and reproduces it on the

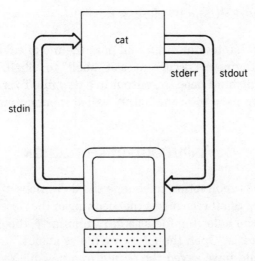

Figure 1.4 A terminal as stdin, stdout, and stderr.

standard output. At first glance, this seems worthless, but if you want to view a file on your terminal all you have to do is type the command:

cat file<return>

The Shell will open the file and reproduce it on stdout (your terminal). Any errors detected, for example, a missing file, will be passed to stderr (again, your terminal).

Some filters extract only the data you want to see while others add or change the data per your instructions. The *grep* command (Globally look for a Regular Expression and Print) will find every occurrence of a word or phrase in a UNIX file. For example, the following command will find all occurrences of my name in a document:

grep "Arthur" chapter1
Author: Lowell Jay Arthur

Only one occurrence was found. *Grep* filtered out all the other lines in the file chapter1. To illustrate how the Shell can use commands to modify and enhance data, imagine that I need to change all occurrences of "shell" to "Shell." The *sed* (stream editor) command is useful:

sed -e "s/shell/Shell/" chapter1

Sed will open chapter1 as stdin and pass the file to stdout (the terminal) while changing all occurrences of "shell" to "Shell." Well, that is certainly useful, but I need the output in a new file. To create a new file with Shell, you need to use a facility called input/output redirection.

7.   INPUT/OUTPUT REDIRECTION

You can use I/O redirection to change the definitions of stdin, stdout, and stderr. The Shell recognizes the meaning of the "less than" symbol (<) as "Open the following file as stdin." Similarly, the "greater than" symbol (>) means "Open the following file as stdout." In the previous example, I could have saved the output in a new file as follows:

sed -e "s/shell/Shell/" chapter1 > newchapter1

The *sed* command knew to open the file, chapter1, as stdin, but I could have also written the command as:

```
sed -e "s/shell/Shell/" < chapter1 > newchapter1
```

But what about stderr? Isn't it still directed to the terminal? Well, yes. Redirecting stderr into a file is only occasionally useful. To do so, however, the Shell recognizes the file descriptor for stderr (2) and the output symbol (>) to mean that stderr should be placed in a file:

```
sed -e "s/shell/Shell/" chapter1 > newchapter1 2> newerrors
```

Any errors will be put in the file newerrors.

Sometimes, it is useful to combine stdout and stderr into one output stream and put it into a single file. To do so is simple:

```
sed -e "s/shell/Shell/" chapter1 2>&1 > newchapter1
```

The expression "2>&1" tells the Shell to duplicate the file descriptor stderr (2) from the descriptor for stdin (1). Then, the Shell redirects both outputs into the file, newchapter1.

Occasionally, you may want to throw away the standard output or the standard error output from a command. UNIX has a bit bucket specially designed for this purpose, /dev/null. It is a device name that the operating system knows as a black hole. Anything directed to it disappears. This is most useful when you do not want to see the diagnostic output from a command; stderr or stdout can be redirected into /dev/null:

```
cmd file 2> /dev/null     # direct stderr into /dev/null
cmd file  > /dev/null      # direct stdout into /dev/null
```

The Shell has two other special features—appending to a file and using part of the Shell command as input—to handle special situations. The output redirection command, ">", creates a new file if the file name does not exist. If the file already exists, the Shell writes over it. Sometimes, it is useful to write some text into a file and then add text to it as required. To do this, you use the symbol to append, ">>". If the file does not exist, the Shell will create it. If it exists, the Shell will append text to the file. A common example involves writing Shell procedures. Often, when using a Shell procedure, you want to create a file of errors and mail them to the person executing the command:

```
echo "First Error" > mailfile
echo "Second Error" >> mailfile
echo "Third Error" >> mailfile
mail lja < mailfile
```

The first error is detected and stored in the mail file. All subsequent errors are appended to the mail file. Finally, the mail is sent to the person executing the command (one message is usually better than three separate ones). You will see other possible uses for appending data in the following chapters.

The remaining redirection device, "<<", uses lines of data *within* the Shell command as input. Using data within the Shell command comes up most often in use with the UNIX editor, *ed*. Rather than having a separate file as input to the command, you can include it directly with the Shell command:

```
ed mailfile <<!
g/Error/s//Terminal Error/
/First/d
w
q
!
```

This command will edit the mail file using the next four lines as input. The Shell input is read up to the occurrence of the exclamation point (!) character. The editor will replace all occurrences of "Error" with "Terminal Error," delete the next occurrence of "First," write the mail file, and quit. This ability is useful when you need to edit more than one file and make the same changes to each.

By the way, you do not have to use the exclamation point: any word will do. For example, you could use "de" ("ed" spelled backwards).

```
ed mailfile <<de
s/Error/Terminal Error/
/First/d
w
q
de
```

Anything else will work equally well.

The C Shell handles input/output redirection almost identically, except for a couple minor exceptions—combining standard output with standard error and overwriting existing files. To combine stderr with stdout, add an ampersand at the end of the redirection sign:

```
command arguments >& outfile
command arguments >>& outfile
```

The output file will contain all the standard output and standard error data created by the shell command.

The C Shell has a variable called *noclobber* that can be set to prevent accidental destruction of existing files. When noclobber is set, it is an error for the output file name to exist. To override this protection, use the exclamation point:

```
command arguments >! outfile
command arguments >&! outfile
command arguments >>! outfile
command arguments >>&! outfile
```

Outfile will be rewritten or appended whether it exists or not. If the variable *noclobber* is not set, the exclamation points are ignored.

Input and output redirection allows you to create files and append to them. It permits the use of existing files as input to the Shell. It allows you to use part of the Shell command as input. It does so without concern for the format of the files, whether they exist or should be created. The Shell handles all of this for you. As you will see in the next chapter, input/output redirection gives you great flexibility to manipulate text.

Sometimes, however, it is unnecessary and somewhat inefficient to create a file for everything. Occasionally, you will want to pass the output of one Shell command to the input of another. Rather than create a file and have the second command read it, you can pass the data from one command to another using the Shell "pipe."

8. PIPES

The "pipe" is exactly what it sounds like—a conduit to carry data from one command to another (Figure 1.5). It connects the stdout of one command to the stdin of another—no messy temporary files to deal with, fewer errors, and greater productivity. Besides eliminating temporary files, the pipe allows the two commands to operate synchronously (at the same time). As soon as the first command creates some output, the second command can begin execution. Figure 1.6 shows the difference in execution time between processes that execute synchronously and asynchronously. The pipe is not only useful but efficient as well.

In a previous example, I changed all occurrences of "shell" to "Shell" in Chapter 1. It might be useful to change all occurrences in all of the chapters and put them into a single file. The pipe (:) would let me combine the *cat* and *sed* commands to do this simply:

cat chapter1 chapter2 chapter3 : sed -e "s/shell/Shell/" > book

Cat concatenates the chapter files and puts them on stdout. The pipe passes the data from the *cat* command to the stream editor command (*sed*), which then edits the data and writes them into the file *book*.

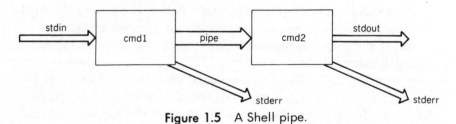

Figure 1.5   A Shell pipe.

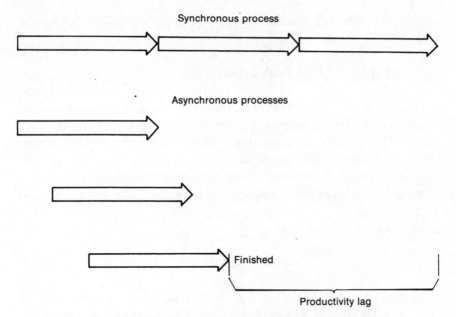

Figure 1.6 Asynchronous versus synchronous processes.

Standard error can be redirected into standard output and then piped into another command as follows:

command arguments 2>&1 ¦ nextcommand

The C Shell handles this more directly:

command arguments ¦& nextcommand

Aside from this minor difference, the Bourne and C Shells both handle pipes in the same way.

Because it may be necessary to save the data passing through a pipe—to test that the correct data is being passed or just to retain the data for future use—there is a facility to save the information in a file. What better name for a pipe fitting than *tee*? *Tee* writes the standard input into a file and onto the standard output. *Tee* is as simple to use as a pipe:

cat chapter? ¦ tee book ¦ nroff -cm

Pipes are used to connect shell commands to perform complex functions and improve efficiency. Rather than coding some new command to handle a needed function, shell commands can be reused, coupled with each other, and shaped to handle even the most difficult text transformations. Information passing through pipes can be saved in files with *tee*. Pipes are a major part of the flexibility and usability of UNIX and Shell.

9. SUMMARY

The simplicity of UNIX files, the file system structure, and the input/output subsystem gives the Shell much of its flexibility and power. Its vast arsenal of reusable commands, or filters, as they are often called, further enhance the power of the Shell. The Shell pipe, by use of synchronous processes, makes commands more efficient and more responsive.

Using the Shell and all its facilities allows users to become more productive, automating the routine tasks to give users time to pursue more creative, fulfilling work.

EXERCISES

1. When should the Shell be used:
    a. interactively?
    b. for programming?

2. Describe UNIX file and file system structures.

3. Diagram and describe a typical Shell filter.

4. What are standard input (stdin), standard output (stdout), and standard error (stderr)?

5. What is input/output redirection?

6. Write a simple interactive Shell using I/O redirection to accept input from file1, put stdout in file2, and stderr in file3.

7. Write a simple Shell to redirect stderr into stdout and put the combined output in outerrfile.

8. Write a simple Shell to append to an existing file.

9. Write a simple Shell, using the pipe, to sort a file both before and after using *grep* to extract information from it. Which form is more efficient?

10. Use *pipe* and *tee* with the previous exercise to put the output of *grep* into a file before sorting the information selected.

2

Shell Commands

Almost any command, with the exception of those run in single-user mode during system start-up, is available to the Shell. This chapter will explain how the Shell finds commands and files. It will also introduce some of the most useful but simplest commands. The commands covered in this chapter are shown in Figure 2.1. Their many uses will be explored further in subsequent chapters.

1. HOW THE SHELL FINDS COMMANDS

Most user Shell commands reside in bins: /bin and /usr/bin. Others, important only to the system administrator, reside in /etc, /usr/rje, and /usr/adm. At system start-up time, commands are available in /stand (stand alone). Users can create their own bin directories for Shell programs (see Chapter 4). For most users, the commands available in /bin and /usr/bin will be of most importance. The /usr/ucb bin contains the Berkeley 4.2 BSD commands.

When a user logs in, the Shell sets up a standard environment using several variables (Figure 2.2). The Shell uses the PATH variable to

cat   —display a file
cd   —change directories
chgrp   —change the group of a file or directory
chmod —change the protections on a file or directory
chown —change the owner of a file or directory
cp   —copy a file
cut   —cut a file apart by fields
dircmp —compare two directories
grep   —select lines of a file by content
ln   —link a file
ls   —list a directory
merge   —put two files together in order
mkdir   —make a directory
mv   —move a file
paste   —put a file or files together
pr   —print a file
pwd   —print working directory
rm   —remove a file
rmdir   —remove a directory
sort   —sort one or more files
sed   —the stream editor
tr   —a character translator

Figure 2.1   Basic Shell commands.

point at each bin that a user can access. The PATH variable is initialized at login time and can be modified using either /etc/profile or the .profile in the user's home directory. In a C Shell system, these variables can be modified in the user's .login or .cshrc files, which reside in the home directory. To find out the default paths available, type the following command:

echo $PATH

The answer in a typical environment will be:

:/bin:/usr/bin:

CDPATH —search path for *cd*
HOME   —path name of the user's login directory
MAIL   —path name of the user's mail file
PATH   —the Shell's search path for commands
PS1   —the primary prompt string:
          "$ " for Bourne Shell systems
          "% " for C Shell systems
PS2   —the secondary prompt string: "> "

Figure 2.2 Shell variables.

meaning that you have all of the standard Shell commands available for execution. The Shell uses this variable to determine where to search for commands and in what order you want to search the bins. The current value of PATH indicates that the Shell will search the current directory, /bin, and /usr/bin. The current directory is represented by a null name, followed by a colon. You can change the order of the search by redefining the value of PATH as follows:

PATH = /usr/bin:/bin::

which reverses the order of the search.

If you had a user bin under your home directory, you might add it to the search path using another Shell variable, HOME:

PATH = ${PATH}:$HOME/bin

Using my login as an example, this would change the value of PATH to:

/usr/bin:/bin::/unix1/lja/bin

Whenever I execute a command, the Shell will look first in /usr/bin, then /bin, the current directory, and finally my user bin. This means that I can type a command name and the Shell will find it; I do not have to type in a full path name to a command I created. This is an important feature of the Shell that helps improve productivity; bins full of user commands can be placed anywhere in the system and accessed directly via the PATH variable.

Because users would rather not change the PATH variable during every session, changes to PATH can be made automatically at login time using the /etc/profile and $HOME/.profile files. The system administrator can redefine PATH to include common user bins by inserting the following two lines into /etc/profile:

```
PATH = :/bin:/usr/bin:/local/bin
export PATH
```

The export command makes the PATH variable available to all subsequent processes initiated by the user.

The user may further modify the PATH variable. You can create the .profile file in your HOME directory and add the following two lines to include your own command bin:

```
PATH = ${PATH}:${HOME}/bin
export PATH
```

These two lines will add your command bin to the Shell's search path. The Shell can now automatically look in all command bins to find any command you request. Problems can occur, however, if there are two commands with the same name in different bin directories; the Shell will execute the first one it finds.

2.   SPECIAL CHARACTERS

The Shell assumes that anything on a command line that is not a command or a flag is a file, directory, or special file. To prevent the user from typing more characters than are necessary and to encourage good naming conventions, the Shell provides the user with special characters (*,?,[...]) to allow automatic substitution of characters in file names. These special characters, sometimes called metacharacters, have the following meanings:

*—matches any string of characters (including none) ·

?—matches any single character

[...]—matches any single character within the brackets

In a previous example, I used the *cat* command to copy the first three chapters of this book into a single file:

    cat chapter1 chapter2 chapter3 > book

This could have been handled more easily in any of the following ways:

    cat ch* > book
    cat chapter? > book
    cat chapter[123] > book

Metacharacters can reduce significantly the keystrokes required to create a series of file names. The drawbacks are few. In the previous example, however, I would have gotten different results if the following files had existed in the directory:

    chapter1 chapter2 chapter3 chapter4 charles

The first command would have concatenated all five files. The second command would have concatenated the first four. Only the last command would have worked exactly as required. Metacharacters can reduce typing effort but can give unexpected results depending on what files are in a directory.

Having covered the basics of finding commands and the use of special characters, we move to the next subject, using simple commands. The simplest commands deal with files and directories.

3.   FILE AND DIRECTORY COMMANDS

The file and directory commands available in /bin and /usr/bin are shown in Figure 2.3. The most elementary file and directory commands

Files	Directories
cat—display a file	ls —list a directory
cp —copy a file	cd —change directories
ln —link a file	dircmp—compare two directories
mv—move a file	mkdir —make a directory
pr —print a file	pwd —print working directory
rm —remove a file	rmdir —remove a directory

chown—change the owner of a file or directory

chgrp —change the group of a file or directory

chmod—change the protections on a file or directory

Figure 2.3 File and directory commands.

are *ls, cd, pwd,* and *cat.* The *ls* (list) command, without any flags or arguments, gives a listing of all of the files and directories in the current directory:

ls
bin
doc
src

The *ls* command can be combined with numerous options, most commonly -l and -ld, to give a more detailed listing of the current directory and its contents:

ls -l

drwxrwx ----	3 lja	adm	992 Dec	1 05:39 bin
drwx ----------	28 lja	adm	496 Dec	4 12:28 doc
drwxr-x -----	2 lja	adm	192 Sep	5 17:55 jcl
drwx ----------	2 lja	adm	816 Sep	5 16:15 job
drwxrwxrwx	2 lja	adm	3760 Dec	3 09:37 rje
drwxrwxrwx	32 lja	adm	1008 Dec	3 18:22 src

ls -ld
drwxrwxrwx   32 lja   adm   437 Dec   3 18:22.

pwd
/unix1/lja

To see all the files in a directory, including those deliberately hidden (by prefacing the file name with period), you should use the -a option:

ls -a
.
..
.cshrc
.login
.profile
bin
doc
src

The *cd* (change directory) command moves the user from one directory to another. You should put related files in different directories to make them easier to find. Proper naming will help you locate files.

Using the *cd* command without any arguments will transfer a user to their home directory. You can use the *pwd* (print working directory) command at any time to determine where you are:

cd
pwd
/unix1/lja

To change to any other directory in the system, you would type:

cd directory_name

For example,

cd src
pwd
/unix1/lja/src

cd /usr/bin
pwd
/usr/bin

The Bourne Shell also uses an environment variable, CDPATH, with the *cd* command to reduce typing. You can set up CDPATH in .profile to include any major directories. Then, no matter where you are in the directory structure, all you have to do is *cd* to the directory name and the Shell remembers where those directories are and changes to them without your doing extensive typing. For example, since you are already in the /usr/bin directory, you could change directory into the *doc* directory by typing:

cd doc

if there was an entry in the .profile as follows:

CDPATH = $HOME/doc
export CDPATH

The directories can also be listed like the PATH variable to give immediate access to any of the major directories:

CDPATH = $HOME/bin:$HOME/doc:$HOME/src
export CDPATH

Using the *cd* command, the user can change from one directory to another without typing long path names. The Shell will print the path name of the directory it has changed into:

cd doc
/unix1/lja/doc

Using the Shell interactively or with actual procedures often requires changing directories. Determining the current directory is also important. Both the *cd* and the *pwd* command can be used anywhere at any time. (This is not entirely true. Users in a restricted Shell [rsh] are prohibited from issuing the *cd* command, but few users ever experience such restrictions.)

The *cat* command, as previously described, takes its arguments, opens the indicated files, and copies them to standard output. *Cat* allows you to display them on your terminal or redirect them into other files:

```
cat .profile
PATH = ${PATH}:${HOME}/bin
export PATH
```

Ls, cd, pwd, and *cat* handle most of the basic file and directory handling needs. They produce their output on stdout, so they can be coupled with other commands via pipes to create more complex commands. Now that files and directories can be viewed, it is important to learn how to extract information from either. The *grep, cut,* and *paste* commands make it easy to select information and prepare it for printing or processing.

4. GREP, CUT, AND PASTE

Every Shell user will need to select, extract, and organize information from files, thereby reducing the information that the user will need to view. The commands to handle this important task are shown in Figure 2.4. *Grep, cut,* and *paste* handle most of the data selection a UNIX user will require.

The *grep* command is important; it finds information in files. It looks for character strings in files and writes the requested information on standard output. I might, for example, want to determine each of the chapters that has the word PATH in it. To do so, I would enter the following command:

Data Selection

awk —a pattern scanning and processing language named after
     its developers, Aho, Kernighan, and Weinberger
cut   —cut a file apart by fields
grep —select lines of a file by content
paste—put a file or files together

Figure 2.4   Data selection commands.

grep PATH *
chapter2: PATH = ${PATH}:${HOME}/bin
chapter2: export PATH

.

.

.

chapter9: the PATH variable.

Unfortunately, *grep* also provided all the lines in each of these files
that contains PATH. To get just the name, I would use:

grep -l PATH *
chapter2
chapter9

Or, I might want to know which lines in the files contain PATH. I
could enter the following command:

grep -n PATH chapter2
28: PATH = $PATH:$HOME/bin
29: export PATH

When looking for strings of more than one word, you must enclose
the string in quotes, otherwise *grep* thinks that the spaces or tabs
between words separate the search string from the file names:

grep -l export PATH *
cannot open PATH

grep -l "export PATH" *
chapter2

There are two other forms of *grep—egrep* and *fgrep—*extended *grep* and fast *grep. Egrep* looks for more than one string at a time while *fgrep* looks for many strings that exactly match a line of the file. These two variations of the command provide efficiency when you are looking for multiple strings in the same files.

Another useful command, word count (*wc*), can count the number of characters, words, and lines in a file. The counts of characters and words are useful for determining a typist's speed and productivity. The number of lines in a file is often useful in Shell programs to determine the scope of a file. Sorts work more efficiently when they know the exact number of lines or records in the file. Also, if a command should create only 10 records instead of 10,000, you can use *wc* to check the outcome of the processing. To find out how many files contain the word PATH:

grep -l PATH chapter? ¦ wc -l
2

Cut and *paste* do exactly what their names suggest—cut files into pieces that can be pasted back together in some other usable fashion. *Cut* can operate on a character-by-character or field-by-field basis or some combination of both. *Paste,* on the other hand, works line by line to put new files together.

One of the simplest examples of using *cut* involves finding a person's name in the /etc/passwd file using just their login name. If you entered the following commands, you would get the lines shown:

who
root
lja

grep lja /etc/passwd
lja:password:user#:group#:Jay Arthur x9999:/unix1/lja:/bin/sh

This is more information than needed. *Cut,* however, can extract the required fields. Fields in /etc/passwd are delimited by a colon (:). Field one is the login name; number two, the password; and so on. All you really need are fields one and five. *Grep* and *cut* can retrieve this information:

grep lja /etc/passwd ¦ cut -f1,5 -d:
lja:Jay Arthur x9999

When creating files using Shell, use delimiters to take advantage of *cut* and *paste.* Most files currently created or maintained in the UNIX system have delimiters to facilitate the use of *cut* and *paste.*

Some of the outputs from commands are not delimited, however. The output of the ls -l command has no delimiters. *Cut* can be used, on a character-by-character basis, to extract only the data required:

ls -l ¦ cut -c1-15,55-
```
drwxrwx ----      3 bin
drwx ---------   28 doc
drwxr-x -----     2 jcl
drwx ---------    2 job
drwxrwxrwx        2 rje
drwxrwxrwx       32 src
```

Using *cut,* you can extract information from a file in any form required. Once the file is cut into several slices, however, you will want to recombine its contents in a different order to present the information in a more usable form. *Paste* can put files together in useful ways.

Paste works on single files, multiple files, or the standard input. Using the *ls* command for example, you can easily create a multiple column listing of a directory's contents:

ls -a ¦ paste - - - -
```
.cshrc       .login      .profile    bin
doc          src
```

The dashes after *paste* tells paste to use one line from standard input in each of those positions. The same result could have been obtained with the following commands:

```
ls -a > dirlist
paste -s -d"\t\t\t\n" dirlist
.cshrc      .login      .profile      bin
doc         src
```

The -s parameter tells *paste* to merge subsequent lines from the same file. The -d parameter tells *paste* to use the characters between the double quotes as delimiters between subsequent lines. In this case, the first three delimiters are tabs(\t); the last delimiter is the newline character(\n). The following command would produce an output with two items per line:

```
paste -s -d"\t\n" dirlist
.cshrc      .login
.profile    bin
doc         src
```

To obtain a more attractive listing, use the print command (*pr*):

```
paste -s -d"\t\n" dirlist ¦ pr -e20
.cshrc      .login
.profile    bin
doc         src
```

or, more simply:

```
ls -a ¦ pr -2 -e20
.cshrc      .login
.profile    bin
doc         src
```

Paste can also put two files together once they have been separated. Using the passwd file, let's extract two of the fields and put them back together in a different order:

```
cut -f1 -d: /etc/passwd > temp1
cut -f5 -d: /etc/passwd > temp2
paste temp2 temp1 > loginlist
pr -e20 loginlist

Jay Arthur x9999      lja
Paula Martin x9999 pgm
```

The secret to making people more productive is to select the right data and present it in a usable format. *Grep, cut,* and *paste* provide a tremendous facility to extract only the data needed, recombine the fields, create a new file, or print the information with another command. *Grep* and *cut* select the data required. *Paste* combines selected data into a usable format. *Cat* or *pr* will print the resulting data. These commands provide the basic tools of a relational database: select and join. It takes a while to gain an understanding of the use and relationships among *grep, cut,* and *paste,* but once acquired, you will wonder how you ever got along without them.

5.   SORT, MERGE, JOIN, AND UNIQ

Having extracted the data, the next logical step is to further refine it using the commands shown in Figure 2.5. In many cases, sorting the data makes the resulting output even easier to use. In other cases, it may be necessary to merge two files that have already been sorted on a common key. The *sort* command performs both of these functions. Sorted output often contains duplicate lines of data; *uniq* will remove them or display only the repeated lines. *Uniq* facilitates the removal or selection of duplicate data—a common requirement in Shell programming.

The *sort* command, as you might have guessed, works on either character positions, fields delimited by tab characters, or some combi-

Data Refinement

join   —relationally join two files
merge—merge one or more files on a specified key
sort   —sort one or many files into a required order
uniq   —identify and print unique or duplicate lines

Figure 2.5 Data refinement commands.

nation of the two. Once again, *sort* is designed to work easily with *grep, cut,* and *paste.* For efficiency, *sort* should be used *after* the data have been selected with *grep* and *cut.* Why sort a whole file, when you can sort a small subset of the total data? For example, I could sort the passwd file by user ID and then extract all the users under the file system /unix1:

sort -t: +0 -1 /etc/passwd ! grep unix1 ! cut -f1 -d:
pgm
lja

This example forces the Shell to sort the entire passwd file and then extract the pertinent information. It would have been more efficient to extract the data and then sort it:

grep unix1 /etc/passwd ! cut -f1 -d: ! sort
lja
pgm

Looking at the previous two examples, you might wonder why the first one had the control flags: +0 −1. These told *sort* to use field 0 as the sort key. Since there was only one field in the second example, no control flags were necessary. Why does *sort* count from field 0 and character 0? I don't know. It has confused more people than it has helped. I presume that because C language counts from 0, *sort* was designed to take advantage of humans instead of the opposite. Figure 2.6 shows a variety of sort commands and the sort keys that will be used.

sort -nr file	sort in reverse numerical order
sort -t: +0 -2 file	sort on fields 1 and 2 delimited by a ":"
sort +0.20 -0.25 file	sort on columns 20-25
sort -rt" " +3 -4 file	sort on field 4 delimited by spaces
sort -m file1 file2	merge file 1 and file 2

Figure 2.6 Various sort commands.

To specify that the fields are delimited by other than a common tab character (HT or, in C language, \t), you must specify the character using the -t option. In the passwd file example, the delimiter was a colon(:). In some files, it may be a blank: -t" ". If there are no consistent field delimiters in the file, use 0.(character position) to identify the start and end positions. To sort a long listing of a directory by the number of characters in each file, in descending (reverse) sequence, use the following command:

```
ls -al ¦ sort -r +0.35n
-rwxr-xr-x      1 lja     adm       12839 Jun 23 05:12 .profile
-rwxr-xr-x      1 lja     adm        4839 Jun 23 05:12 .cshrc
-rwxr-xr-x      1 lja     adm        4139 Jun 23 05:12 .login
drwxrwxrwx     32 lja     adm        1008 Dec  3 18:22 src
drwxrwx ----    3 lja     adm         992 Dec  1 05:39 bin
drwx ---------  28 lja    adm         496 Dec  4 12:28 doc
```

Sort can organize any UNIX file by fields or characters. Occasionally, the need arises to combine two or more files that are already sorted. In these cases, it is more efficient to merge the files. The output of the *ls* command, for example, is already sorted. To get a sorted listing of the commands available to a UNIX user under the /bin and /usr/bin directories, the following commands would provide equivalent outputs:

```
ls /bin > binlist
ls /usr/bin > usrbinlist
sort binlist usrbinlist > cmdlist
```

```
ls /bin > binlist
ls /usr/bin ! sort -m binlist - > cmdlist
```

Since merging is more efficient than sorting, the second set of commands is preferable. The second command uses the dash (-) to tell *sort* to look for one of its inputs on standard input (the output of "ls /usr/bin"). This eliminates one temporary file, another efficiency consideration. The file, cmdlist, can now be printed with *pr* or included in a memo or user guide.

As previously mentioned, problems can occur when there are duplicate command names in /bin, /usr/bin, and user bins. To identify these potential problems, you could compare the three listings of /bin, /usr/bin, and $HOME/bin manually. This is nothing but drudgery and is susceptible to error. It can be automated using *join,* which reads two files as input and puts out a single file containing a "join" of only those lines from both files that match on a specified field (normally the first and, in this case, the command names):

```
ls /bin > binlist
ls $HOME/bin > homebinlist
join binlist homebinlist
cat
sort
```

Sort and *uniq* can automate this analysis when more than two files are involved:

```
ls /bin > binlist
ls /usr/bin > usrbinlist
ls $HOME/bin > homebinlist
sort -m binlist usrbinlist homebinlist ! uniq -d
cat
sort
```

Two commands, *cat* and *sort,* are duplicated in two of the three
directories. These could be easily located:

```
egrep cat\:sort *binlist
binlist:cat
binlist:sort
homebinlist:cat
homebinlist:sort
```

Similarly, *uniq* could have been used to create a merged listing of
the three directories, excluding all duplicate command names:

```
sort -m binlist usrbinlist homebinlist : uniq > cmdlist
```

In other instances, use *uniq* to show only those lines that are not
repeated. When comparing two directories that should have identical
contents, the only concern is identifying the files unique to each directory. To list them, use the following command:

```
ls dir1 > dir1list
ls dir2 : sort -m dir1list - : uniq -u > differences
```

or, more simply:

```
dircmp dir1 dir2
```

Sort, merge, join, and *uniq* are powerful tools for manipulating information and preparing it for human consumption. Combined with
cut and *paste,* they provide a marvelous facility to automate the common functions of data selection and sorting. The remaining needs of a
Shell programmer are to transform or translate the information into
another form, and to print the results.

6. TRANSFORMERS AND TRANSLATORS

There are three main facilities for transforming or translating data
(Figure 2.7): *sed* (the stream editor), *tr* (translator), and *newform* (or

Data Translators

newform—change tabs in a file
sed   —edit a stream of data using editor commands
tr   —translate a stream of data using tables

Figure 2.7 Data transformers and translators.

reform for versions prior to Version V). *Sed* transforms incoming data by executing editor commands on the standard input. *Tr* translates incoming data, character by character, based on conversion tables specified by the user. *Newform* transforms files based on the input and output tab specifications.

Sed is used in pipes in place of the standard line editor (*ed*). For simple substitutions, the editor commands can be put on the command line:

    sed -e "s/shell/Shell/" chapter1 > newchapter1

For more complex transformations involving many substitutions, you can put the editor commands in a file and specify them as input to *sed:*

    sed -f sedfile chapter1 > newchapter1

where sedfile contains the following:

    s/shell/Shell/
    s/c language/C Language/

Sed is an efficient method of transforming a file into some other usable format. For example, the output of the word count command (*wc*) looks like this:

    wc -l file
       35 file

File has 35 lines in it. Using *sed,* the numbers can be extracted by removing blanks, tabs, and the characters "a-z" as follows:

```
wc -l file : sed -e "s/[ \ta-z][ \ta-z]*//g"
35
```

The translate command (*tr*) works similarly to the *sed* command, but it changes the standard input, character by character rather than string by string. *Sed* operates on strings, but is hard to use on a character-by-character basis. Use the following command to translate a file from uppercase into lowercase:

```
tr "[A-Z]" "[a-z]" < uppercase > lowercase
```

The expression "[A-Z]" signifies the uppercase letters from A to Z. The second expression "[a-z]" tells *tr* to substitute the lowercase letters, on a one-for-one basis, with the uppercase letters. Doing this with *sed* would take a file with 26 editor commands; tr is much simpler.

Tr can also be used in other situations that require transformations. If I wanted to change chapter one into a file of just words and obtain a sorted listing of the words and the number of times they were used, I could issue the following command:

```
tr "[ ]" "[\012]" < chapter1 : sort : uniq -c
```

In this example, *tr* translates blanks into newline (\012) characters (one word per line). These are then sorted in alphabetical order and counted by *uniq*. This output would show all of the words in the document and the number of times they occur. It can be used to identify overused words that should be varied to improve the quality of the prose.

Similarly, to convert a file delimited by colons(:) to a file delimited by tab characters, you could use either of the following commands:

```
sed -e "s/:/\t/g" < colonfile > tabfile
tr "[:]" "[\t]" < colonfile > tabfile
```

The *newform* command (or *reform* on older systems) serves the purpose of changing the meaning of embedded tab characters. For example, to conserve space on a UNIX system, as much white space as possible should be removed from files before storing them. This provides more efficient disk storage as well as telecommunications. *Newform* can translate files with extensive blank characters into a compressed version that takes advantage of tab characters.

In most UNIX systems, tabs are set to one every eight characters:

```
00000000011111111112222222222333333333344444444445555555555
12345678901234567890123456789012345678901234567890123456789 0
     T       T        T          T         T         T         T
```

To take advantage of the data compression allowed by the use of tab characters, *newform* can translate the old file into "dash eight" tabs as follows:

```
newform -i-0 -o-8 < oldfile > tabfile
reform -0 -8 < oldfile > tabfile (Versions 3.0 and before)
```

It specifies the input tab format of none (-0) and an output format of eight (-8). In many cases, the size of a file will be reduced by a third or more. Many more transformations are possible and will be introduced in subsequent chapters.

Both *sed* and *tr* are useful for translating and transforming a file or input stream. *Sed* is stronger for use with strings, words, or lines. *Tr* is stronger when operating on characters. *Newform* and *reform* handle conversion of files with tab characters. Each plays an integral part in the use of the Shell.

7. EDITORS

UNIX editors (and there are a slew of them, see Figure 2.8) are also commands available to the Shell. The next few sections will discuss the use of editors with the Shell. The specifics of using each editor have been left out because editor usage varies from installation to installation.

UNIX Editors

ed   —line editor
emacs—a screen editor
se   —another screen editor
vi   —a "visual" editor

Figure 2.8   UNIX editors.

Sometimes, it is not possible to *grep, cut, paste, sed,* or *tr* a file into a required format. A few lines may have to be added to a file or human analysis will be needed. In these cases, you can use the editor of your choice from within a Shell command. Editors are an important tool for manipulating text. When used repetitively within a Shell procedure, they become more beneficial.

7.1. *Ed*

As previously described, the standard UNIX line editor (*ed*) can use commands typed in-line as follows:

```
ed file <<!
/First/
a
These are the times that try men's souls
And mine too for that matter.
.
w
q
!
```

This would find the line with the first occurrence of "First" and append the next two lines after that line. This facility is occasionally useful in Shell commands.

7.2.   Vi, se, emacs, and Other Editors

From the terminal, *vi* or any of the other editors can be invoked interactively. They can also be used in Shell commands to present a file
to a user for editing:

vi chapter?

8.   PRINTING

The previous sections have discussed various ways of selecting information from files, translating the information into other forms, and
sorting the information into a meaningful order. These are the essential steps in preparing information for use. The final step displays the
information on the user's screen or printer.

All of the Shell commands have stdout and stderr files that can be
displayed on the screen or a printer. The output of these can be redirected into files or devices. But these outputs are rarely formatted for
easy human consumption. The facilities for formatting output are *pr*,
nroff, and *awk.*

Pr prints files with simple headings and page breaks. Where *cat* lists
a file exactly as it exists, *pr* provides the file name and date of last
modification in the title and provides facilities to break the output
every so many lines for clarity. The command line to print a C-
language file on a 66-line printer would be:

pr -o8 file.c

The same command to display the file on a 25-line terminal screen
and pause between pages would be:

pr -l24 -p -t -w79 file.c

To print a file, delimited by colons(:), with a special heading and 20-
character width fields:

pr -e:20 -h "Special Report" file

Nroff formats documents using *nroff* and *mm* macros, but it can be used with files whose fields are delimited by unique characters, like the password file. *Tbl,* the table preprocessor, creates the input to *nroff.*
    Tbl requires a text file like the following:

```
.TS
tab(:) ;                    tablestart
I I n n I I I.
text file
.TE                      ___ tableend
```

The password file can be formatted with *tbl* and *nroff* as follows:

tbl tablestart /etc/passwd tableend ¦ nroff

And for those users with even more rigorous reporting requirements, *awk* provides many of the capabilities of C language. It allows
variable definition and control flow, but is interpretive and therefore
more responsive to the user's needs than compiling and testing C-
language programs.
    The previous example could have been written in *awk* as follows:

```
{
BEGIN { FS = ":" }
printf "%-3s %.4d %.4d %-35s %s\n", $1, $3, $4, $5, $6
}
```

Assume this file is called awkpasswd. "$1" represents the first field in
the passwd file; "$2", the second; and so on. The format shown follow-
ing the printf statement uses the same conventions of the C-language
printf statement. These can be found in section 3 of the *UNIX User's
Manual.* The command to print the file would be:

awk -f awkpasswd /etc/passwd

Awk uses the awkpasswd file as the program to process the file /etc/passwd. The resulting output would be:

lja   1   1   Jay Arthur x9999 /unix1/lja
pgm   2   2   Paula Martin x9999 /unix1/pgm

Awk, pr, and *nroff* give the user a variety of ways of printing information already selected and sorted by the commands described earlier in this chapter. These formatted reports simplify human interaction with UNIX and are desirable. Humans are only as good as the information presented and its format.

9.   SECURITY

Security is an important feature of UNIX and the Shell. You can create files and by setting the permissions allow people to read, write, or execute your file. The permissions are established in binary as shown in Figure 2.9. Two commands affect the accessibility of a file: *umask* and *chmod.* The long form of the *ls* command (*ls* -l) will display the accessibility of any file or directory *that the user can read.*

There are three levels of security: what the owner of the file can do, what his or her related group can do, and what the world can do. The different levels or modes are also shown in Figure 2.9.

The *umask* command sets up the default security for any file or directory created. The default security for a file is 666 (read and write permission for everyone). The default security for a directory is 777 (read, write, and execute). Without the execute bit, directories cannot be searched. The *umask* command tells the operating system which permissions to exclude when creating a new file or directory. The *umask* command is executed at login time by either /etc/profile, $HOME/.profile, $HOME/.cshrc, or $HOME/.login. The most common *umask* command is:

umask 022

which means omit write permission for the user's group and the world. Everyone can read your files or directories, but no one can write in or

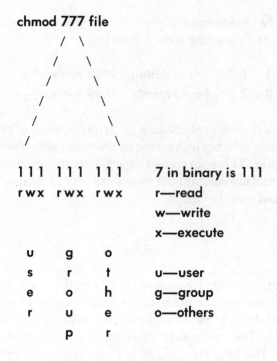

Figure 2.9 File security.

over them. If you want to keep the world out of your files, put the following command in your .profile:

> umask 027

which lets your group read your files or directories, but prohibits any other user from accessing your files in any way.

Once the file or directory has been created with default security, you will occasionally need to change the permissions. The change mode command (*chmod*) allows you to do so:

> chmod 755 shellcommand
> chmod +x shellcommand

When you write a Shell command with one of the editors, the file is normally created with read and write permissions, but not execute. To make the file executable, you must change the permissions as shown. To ensure that only you or your group may execute the command, you would enter:

```
chmod 750 shellcommand
chmod ug+x,o-rwx shellcommand
```

Sometimes you will create an important file that you do not want to delete. The remove command (*rm*) will remove anything for which you have write permission. To get *rm* to ask you before it removes the important file, you can change the file's mode:

```
chmod 444 importantfile
chmod -w importantfile

rm *
rm: importantfile mode 444 ?
```

The *umask* and *chmod* commands allow control of file and directory access. Changing permissions is necessary and continuous in a UNIX environment. Making files executable is another important part of creating Shell commands.

10. SUMMARY

Shell commands are usually found in a directory named bin. The most frequently used directories are /bin and /usr/bin. As a user or toolsmith develops new Shell tools, these commands can be placed in local bins that can be addressed directly via the PATH variable.

The most commonly used file and directory commands are *ls, cd, cat,* and *grep.* The output of each command has been structured to maximize its utility when combined with other commands (e.g., *cut, paste, uniq,* and *pr*) that select portions of their output and report the information required.

Ordering the output in a meaningful way is the job of *sort,* which handles both sorting and merging information. The *join* command also can be used to integrate information from two different files.

Once output files have been created, the information they contain can be translated by *sed* or *tr*. *Sed* operates on strings of information; *tr* operates on characters.

More complex transformations that require operator intervention can be handled by using the UNIX editors. These can be invoked directly from the Shell or Shell procedures.

The output of these commands can be formatted for ease of use with the *awk*, *pr*, and *nroff* commands. Each of these commands can work on files of lines and the fields within those lines. *Awk* and *pr*, in particular, are good for prototyping report programs. *Awk* allows the user to create detailed reports that are not as easily generated using the other two commands.

These basic commands are the roots of more advanced usage of the Shell. Understanding how they interact with each other via the pipe or by input/output redirection is essential to advanced Shell usage. To maximize their benefits, however, requires an understanding of the five Shell control structures described in Chapter 3.

EXERCISES

1. Describe the importance of PATH and CDPATH.

2. Describe the use of the Shell metacharacters:
   a. *
   b. ?
   c. [...]

3. Given a directory containing the following files,

   Abel, Cain, George, Gorth, Greg, Sam, Ted, Tod

   use the *ls* command to list only those files:
   a. consisting of three letters,
   b. consisting of four letters,
   c. that begin with a *G* followed by *e* or *o*,
   d. that begin with *T* and end with *d*.

4. Describe the *ls, pwd,* and *cat* commands.

5. Describe the *grep, cut,* and *paste* commands.

6. Describe the use of *sort, merge, join,* and *uniq.*

7. Name the different Shell translation commands and the type of data (strings, characters, delimiters) each is best designed to handle.

8. Describe the usage of *umask* and *chmod.* How do they offer security in a UNIX file system?

9. Write a Shell to extract, sort, and print all users in the *global* file system. (Use the /etc/passwd file as input.)

10. Using the Shell from the last exercise, extract only those users with multiple entries in the /etc/passwd file.

11. Write a Shell to translate the /etc/passwd file into uppercase and translate the ":" delimiters into tab characters.

12. Write the *umask* command to prohibit all other users (except the owner) from accessing files created by the user. Write the *chmod* commands to make Shell programs executable by:
   a. the owner,
   b. the owner and his or her group,
   c. the world.

13. Write the *pr* command to print the /etc/group file on the user's screen and printer.

14. Write a simple *awk* command to print the same information from the /etc/group file as in the previous problem.

CHAPTER

3

Shell
Control Structures

The chapters to this point have provided information about using simple Shell commands. To make full use of the Shell, however, requires the use of a special set of Shell commands that control what happens and when. These commands allow the user to decide among two different actions (IF-THEN-ELSE), many actions (CASE), and looping through a single action many times (DO WHILE and DO UNTIL). All third-generation programming languages have these basic control structures: IF-THEN-ELSE, CASE, DO WHILE, and DO UNTIL.

Even the most sophisticated fourth-generation languages use these control structures. The Shell provides the most common ones necessary to write structured procedures: IF-THEN-ELSE, CASE, FOR, UNTIL, and WHILE. The C Shell offers a slightly different, but equivalent, set of control structures: IF-THEN-ELSE, SWITCH, FOREACH, WHILE, and REPEAT. Each of the Bourne Shell commands—*if, then, else, elif,*

47

fi, case, esac, for, while, until, do, and *done*—are only recognized if they are the first word on a command line, thus enforcing a structured one-command-per-line programming style. The examples in this chapter will demonstrate this more clearly. There is a single device that handles all the conditions for each of these control structures: *test.* The Shell also provides mechanisms for executing repetitive commands interactively: *xargs* and *find.* Each of these control structures permits loops and decisions to be made by Shell procedures. There is a way to handle interruptions—breaks, deletes, rubouts, and hangups—named *trap.* Properly written, Shell procedures need never fail because they can always take a reasonable default action using *trap.* The ability to test conditions and take actions is the most important feature of the Shell command language.

1. TEST

At the heart of each control structure is a conditional test. The *test* command can determine whether a given name is a file or directory; whether it is readable, writable, or executable; and whether two strings or integers are greater than, less than, or equal to each other. Features of *test* also allow AND, OR, and NOT logic. Figure 3.1 shows all of the basic comparisons available with *test.*

The Shell provides a number of predefined variables that are used frequently. They are described in Figure 3.2. TEST, like any other Shell command, always returns a true or false value in the Shell variable $?. All Shell commands should return a zero (0) when successful and a nonzero value (usually 1 or −1) when they fail. For C-language programmers, this is confusing because FALSE is zero and TRUE is nonzero. So, C-language programmers will have to ignore the return code and focus on the TRUE/FALSE logic.

If a file exists and it is readable, the result is TRUE (0):

```
test -r filename
echo $?
0
```

-b file —file is a block special file
-c file —file is a character special file
-d file —file exists and is a directory
-f file —file exists and is a file
-g file —file has the set-group-id bit set
-k file —file has the sticky bit set
-p file —file is a named pipe
-r file —file is readable
-s file —file is greater than 0 bytes in length
-t n   —n is a file descriptor associated with a terminal
-u file —file has the set-user-id bit set
-w file—file is writable
-x file —file is executable

string   —string is not the null string
-n string—string has a non-zero length
-z string—string has a length of zero
string1 = string2 —string1 equals string2
string1 != string2—string1 not equal to string2

integer1 -eq integer2—algebraic equality
        -ne
        -gt
        -ge
        -lt
        -le

! —NOT operator
-a—AND operator
-o—OR operator

Figure 3.1 Comparisons for test.

$CDPATH —search path for *cd*
$HOME   —path name of the user's login directory
$MAIL   —path name of the user's mail file
$PATH   —the Shell's search path for commands
$PS1   —the primary prompt string:
              "$ " for Bourne Shell systems
              "% " for C Shell systems
$PS2   —the secondary prompt string: "> "

$#   —the number of positional parameters on the command
              line
$-   —the flags supplied to the Shell
$?   —the return code from the previous command
$$ —the current process number
$!   —the process number of the last background command

Figure 3.2   Shell variables.

Similarly, if two strings are not equal, TEST returns a FALSE (nonzero):

test "myname" = "lja"
echo $?
1

Under the Bourne Shell, *test* can be written by enclosing the conditions in square brackets. The C Shell uses parentheses:

Bourne Shell	C Shell
if ["myname" = "lja"]	if (-r filename)

Either of these versions is preferable to using *test* because they make the control structures easier to read. The readability becomes apparent when looking at any of the control structures: IF-THEN-ELSE, CASE,

DO WHILE, or DO UNTIL. More on using these with *test* in the following sections.

Most tests will be performed on variable names created in the Shell. Thus use of the control structures will also depend on the use of variables.

2.   VARIABLES

The Shell lets you establish variables to hold values while you process them. It provides several standard variables (Figure 3.2) that are always accessible.

You can establish your own variables by simply assigning values to variable names:

Bourne Shell	C Shell
tempname = /usr/tmp	set tempname = /usr/tmp
month = 01	set month = 01

To access these variables, you insert the variable name (preceded by a dollar sign) wherever you need it:

```
cp file $tempname
echo "Current month is $month"
```

To be perfectly accurate and prevent errors, you should enclose the name in braces:

```
cp file ${tempname}
echo "Current month is ${month}"
```

Otherwise, establishing other variable names can lead to problems when the Shell tries to interpret your commands:

```
temp=/tmp/
echo $tempname
```

Should the Shell echo "/tmp/name" or "/usr/tmp"? Probably the second one, but the answer would have been obvious had you used either of the following:

echo ${temp}name
/tmp/name
echo ${tempname}
/usr/tmp

Shell variables can be changed throughout the execution of a Shell command, allowing looping and testing without repeating the logic many times. The examples in the following sections should help clarify the benefits and usage of Shell variables.

3.   IF-THEN-ELSE

Often you will want to test whether a file exists before taking one of two actions. The simplest way to make a TRUE/FALSE test is with the IF-THEN-ELSE (Figure 3.3). Bourne and C Shell versions of the IF-

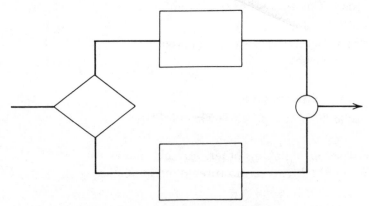

Figure 3.3   IF-THEN-ELSE flowchart.

THEN-ELSE are almost identical. There are two forms of the IF-THEN-ELSE:

```
if [ test conditions ]      if [ test conditions ]
then                        then
  process1                    process1
else                        fi
  process2
fi
```

The default processing path of the second example does nothing. In most cases, however, you will want to take one of two actions. If a file exists, for example, you might want to print it on the screen. If not, you might want to create it. A simple test to do so would look like this:

```
if [ -r filename ]
then
  cat filename
else
  echo "Enter the data for filename"
  cat > filename
fi
```

Some Shell commands will run in the background, without user interaction. They may also be run interactively. To test whether to send messages to the terminal or to mail them to the user (rather than interrupting what the user is currently doing), you could include the following logic in your Shell:

```
if [ -t 0 ]       # (If the standard input is a terminal)
then
  echo "Error Message"
else              # (the command is running in background)
  echo "Error Message" ¦ mail ${LOGNAME}
fi
```

You may also test whether a parameter has a value and take an action:

```
if [ "$PATH" ]
then
   echo $PATH
else
   echo "No path is specified"
fi
```

Test automatically assumes that if there are no parameters it should return a FALSE exit status. This test is particularly useful when applied to user-created variables and parameters.

The Bourne Shell offers a feature that the C Shell does not—an operator to nest IF-THEN-ELSE constructs, *elif,* which is useful for implementing CASE control structures.

```
if [ -d $variable ]
then
   process directory $variable
elif [ -f $variable ]
then
   process file $variable
else
   error
fi
```

The IF-THEN-ELSE is useful for two-path decisions and nested tests of the form shown, but to test a variable for more than one value, use the CASE construct.

4.   CASE AND SWITCH

Frequently a Shell command will create variables or receive parameters that can have many different values. Although the IF-THEN-

ELSE can be used to test each of these values and take action, the
CASE control structure (Figure 3.4) is more convenient. It has the
following forms:

Bourne Shell	C Shell
case $variable in	switch ($variable)
value1)	case value1:
action1	action1
;;	breaksw
value2)	case value2:
action2	action2
;;	breaksw
value3¦value4)	case value3:
	case value4:
action3	action3
;;	breaksw
*)	default:
default action	default action
;;	breaksw
esac	endsw

The last test, "*)", is a default action; if no other value matches, then
the default action is taken. Often, you will need to issue an error
message and exit from the Shell without doing anything. CASE structures are particularly useful for processing parameters to the procedure. For example, the Shell variable, $#, contains a count of the
number of parameters passed to a Shell command. When working interactively, $# is zero (0). When using a Shell command, the value can
run from zero to several hundred. Most Shell commands require some
parameters (at least a file to operate on) as information to begin pro-

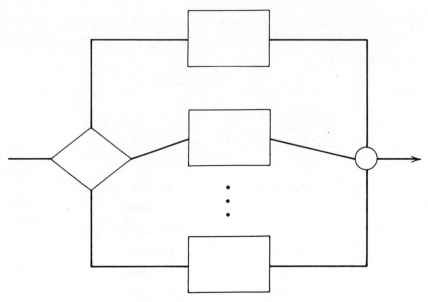

Figure 3.4 CASE flowchart.

cessing. $# should be greater than zero. To test for the number of parameters, use the *case* command and $#:

```
case $# in
    0)
        echo "Enter file name:"
        read argument1
        ;;
    1)
        argument1=$1
        ;;
    *)
        echo "Invalid number of arguments provided to Shell"
        echo "Syntax: command filename"
        exit 1
        ;;
esac
# main processing begins here
```

Assume for a moment that you use Shell to create a monthly report and that the processing differs from month to month. To test and properly execute the command, use the *date* command and test for each of the months:

```
case `date '%m'` in
    01)
            January
            ;;
    02)
            February
            ;;

    .

    .

    .

    12)
            December
            ;;
    *)
            echo "Problems with the date command"
            ;;
esac
```

January, February, and so on are the actual names of commands that have to be executed. The characters surrounding the date command are called accent graves. They tell the Shell to execute the command in a sub-Shell and to put the resulting value in place of the command. So, the date command returns only the month (%m) and the Shell executes the command line:

```
case 01 in
```

for January.

The CASE control structure can also be used for character strings.

Multiple character strings can be specified to default to the same action:

```
case $currentdate in
  01|Jan|January)
     January
     ;;
  02|Feb|February)
     February
     ;;

     .

     .

     .

esac
```

The *case* and *switch* commands are a powerful way of handling many comparisons and many different actions. Sometimes, however, an action needs to be repeated using different files or different information. The commands to handle repetitive operations are *for, while,* and *until.*

5.   FOR AND FOREACH

The *for* (Bourne Shell) and *foreach* (C Shell) control structures (Figure 3.5) permit looping through a series of actions while changing a variable name specified on the *for* command line. Both interactively and in

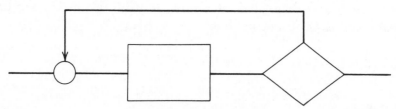

Figure 3.5   FOR flowchart.

a background mode, the use of Shell will require processing many different files the same way. The common form of the *for* and *foreach* structures are as follows:

Bourne Shell	C Shell
for variable in value1 value2	foreach variable value1...
do	repeat action
repeat action on $variable	end
done	

To edit all of the files for this book, replacing "shell" with "Shelf," I could use the following commands:

```
for file in chapter*
do
ed - $file <<!
g/shell/s//Shell/g
w
q
!
done
```

This could also be done for files with many different names:

```
for file in file1 filename xyz etc
```

FOR control structures, as well as any Shell control structures, can be nested inside of one another. For example, to process all the files in the directories bin, doc, and src, I could use the following nested control structure:

```
for dir in bin doc src
do
   cd $dir
   for file in *
   do
```

```
    if [ -f $file ]
    then
        process $file
    fi
  done
  cd ..
done
```

For each of the directories, the Shell would change into that directory. Then, for each file it would test to ensure that the variable $file is really a file and not a directory, and then the Shell would execute the command "process" on each file name. When the Shell finished with all the files under bin, it would change up to the parent directory and then start working on the doc directory. Nesting control structures is a convenient way to handle complex operations that would require extensive typing to accomplish the same ends.

The *for* command is not the only way to handle looping through repetitive operations. The *while* and *until* commands provide another alternative.

6. WHILE AND UNTIL

The *while* command (Figure 3.6) takes a form similar to the *for* command:

Bourne Shell	C Shell
while command list	while (expression)
do	repetitive actions
repetitive actions	end
done	

Sometimes you will need to start an infinite loop. The *test* command recognizes the existence of any value as TRUE:

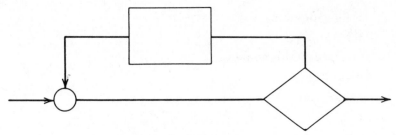

Figure 3.6   WHILE flowchart.

```
while [ 1 ]
do
    process something
done
```

To prevent looping forever or forcing the user to break out of the loop by using one of the break or delete keys, you will need to break out of the loop. The *break* command, as shown in the following example, is the way to jump out of a loop without causing logic problems.

```
while [ 1 ]
do
    if [ end condition ]
    then
       break
    else
       process something
    fi
done
```

Sometimes the processing will need to continue without processing anything. The *continue* handles these requirements:

```
while [ 1 ]
do
    echo "Enter file name"
    read filename
```

```
      if [ -r $filename ]
      then
         process $filename
      else
         continue
      fi
   done
```

The *while* command can also use *test* on variable names and files, processing them accordingly:

```
   while [ "$variable" ]
   do
      process $variable
   done

   while [ -r $file ]
   do
      process $file
   done
```

The *until* form of the loop (Figure 3.7), only available with the Bourne Shell, is used less often. It executes the processing at least once and then tests the conditions.

```
   until [ end conditions ]        until `who ! grep lja`
   do                              do
      processing                      sleep 60
   done                            done
```

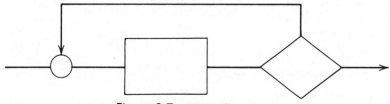

Figure 3.7   UNTIL flowchart.

This *until* example is useful when watching for known hackers to enter the system under a specific ID. A generalized hacker check could watch for the user's ID to appear on the system and then send mail and call the system administrator:

```
# Hacker Check
until `who ! grep $1`
do
    sleep 60
done
echo `date` there's a hacker in the machine ! mail lja
# call my office phone (or home phone)
cu 5551234
```

The C Shell also includes the *repeat* form of loop, which executes a command a specified number of times:

```
repeat 10 command
```

Aside from the *for, foreach, while, until,* and *repeat,* there are a few other ways to handling loops and process many files: *xargs* and *find.*

7. XARGS AND FIND

The Shell provides two other facilities for handling repetitive operations: *xargs* and *find. Xargs* takes lines of input and executes commands, substituting the input lines wherever specified. *Find* searches downward from a specified directory and can execute commands, substituting file or directory names into the command. *Xargs* is useful when interactively executing the same command on many files in a directory. *Find* is more useful for examining entire file structures in background and executing commands.

Some Shell commands, like remove (*rm*), only work on a maximum number of files (100). Since the command

```
rm *
```

results in an error message when there are more than 100 files, *xargs* can be used to execute the *rm* command with the first 100 and then the remaining files:

```
ls ┊ xargs -n100 rm -f
```

Similarly, a series of existing files can be copied to other names:

```
ls chapter* ┊ xargs -i cp { } old{ }
```

This command creates a duplicate set of the chapters from a book named oldchapter1, etc. Instead of creating duplicate copies, however, it would be better to store each of the chapters in the Source Code Control System (SCCS):

```
ls chapter* ┊ xargs -i admin -n -i{ } $HOME/doc/sccs/book/s.{ }
```

This command stores the chapters in the directory $HOME/doc/sccs/ book for later retrieval and update.

Xargs simplifies the implementation of loops when you only need to execute one command with a list of files. The problem is more complicated when every file under a user's ID must be examined or when entire file systems must be changed. The *find* command has the ability to look through entire directory trees for specific files or directories and then execute commands on those file or directory names.

A common occurrence is for a user to change from one work group to another. To allow other members of their group to access a file, they could either change each file and directory one at a time, or they could use *find:*

```
cd $HOME
find . -exec chgrp newgrp { } \;
```

which says find all of the files and directories under my login and change the group ownership of each one to the new group. The braces indicate where the *find* command should substitute the name of each file and directory found during its search. The same ability can be used

to change the mode on all of the files or to copy the files from one place
to another:

```
cd $HOME/bin
find . -exec chmod 775 { } \;
find . -print ¦ cpio -pd new_place
```

Find can also test each name and take action. To change mode on all
of the directories under the login directory, you could use:

```
cd $HOME
find . -type d -exec chmod 770 { } \;
```

Find can even ask you if it is okay to execute the command:

```
find . -type d -ok chmod 770 { } \;
```

The option *-ok* works just like *-exec* except that *find* will prompt you
before executing the command.

Once again, use *xargs* when working on many files generated from a
list command or a file of names; use *find* to operate on all of the directories and files under a specific directory. They both work well when
using the Shell interactively.

8.   TRAP

Finally, the *trap* command provides the ability to handle interrupts:
phone lines hanging up, breaks, deletes, kill commands, virtually anything. Each of these is a signal described in section 2 of the *UNIX
User's Manual* under *signal*(2). The available signals are shown in
Figure 3.8.

Most often, when the Shell receives an interrupt, you will want to
remove all temporary files and exit gracefully with a return code. This
is accomplished by executing the following command:

```
trap (rm tmp*;exit 1) 1 2 3 14 15
```

1—hangup
2—interrupt
3—quit
4—illegal instruction
5—trace trap
6—IOT instruction
7—EMT instruction
8—floating point exception
9—kill (cannot be trapped)
10—bus error
11—segmentation violation
12—bad argument to system call
13—write on a pipe with no receiving process
14—alarm clock
15—software termination signal
16—user defined signal1
17—user defined signal2
18—death of a child process
19—power failure

Figure 3.8   Error signals.

When the Shell receives a hang-up, interrupt, quit, alarm, or software termination signal, it will remove the temporary files (rm tmp*) and exit with a false value (exit 1). In cases where the command is working on many files and you would like to know where to restart the command:

trap (echo ${filename} > stopfile; exit 0) 1 2 3 14 15

Stopfile will contain the name of the last file used by the command.

These are simple examples, but every Shell command should clean up after itself and take some meaningful action when interrupted. *Trap* encourages the active rather than passive handling of signals.

9. SUMMARY

The Shell provides many facilities for controlling actions. The use of repetitive control structures like *for, until, while, xargs,* and *find* will improve your productivity. The *test, if-then-else, case,* and *trap* commands each help improve the reliability and usability of your commands. The Shell control structures are the foundation of good Shell programming. Use them wisely and productively.

They can be used productively in two ways: interactively at the terminal and as the basis for interactive and batch commands that automate much of a UNIX user's work. These subjects will be explored more fully in Chapters 4 and 5.

EXERCISES

1. Name the control structures in the Bourne and C Shells and describe their use.

2. What Shell facility handles all conditional tests for the Shell control structures? Which Shell variable contains the return code from a conditional test?

3. What other Shell commands can be used to handle repetitive processes?

4. What Shell facility handles errors and interrupts?

5. Write the IF-THEN-ELSE statement to test whether a variable name is a directory. Write the same test for file names.

6. Write a CASE statement to test a variable name for the values: "data", "source", "comments", or anything else.

7. Write a FOR loop to process all of the *files* in a directory.

8. Write an infinite loop to prompt the terminal user to input file names which are to be removed, and then remove them. Use *trap* to exit gracefully when finished.

9. Write an infinite loop to check a directory for files, print them using *pr* if any are found, remove them after printing, and then sleep for 15 minutes (900 seconds).

10. Use *xargs* to process all of the files in a directory.

11. Use *find* to locate all of the files in a user's ID named *.c (C-language source code) and print them with *pr*.

12. Write the *trap* statements to handle:
    a. ignoring hang-up signals,
    b. removing temporary files when QUIT or INTERRUPT are received,
    c. removing temporary files when the command ends normally.

CHAPTER

4

======================

Interactive
Shell Usage

One of the most productive ways to use the Shell is interactively at the terminal. Most of the time, you will not need to set up elaborate Shell procedures to do what needs to be done. Why waste the time developing a special program to handle it? Just use the Shell interactively.

When creating a Shell program (as described in Chapter 5), you will often use the Shell interactively to *prototype* or test out how the command will ultimately work. Thus interactive use of the Shell will also serve the development of procedures.

1. USING SHELL AT THE TERMINAL

Anytime you execute any command (e.g., *ls, cat,* or *who*), you are using the Shell interactively: standard input, output, and error are all directed to the terminal. Combining commands via the *pipe* or executing existing Shell programs all contribute to productive use of UNIX through interactive use of the Shell.

You should use the Shell interactively whenever you need immediate results (list a directory with *ls*), or you will have to interact with the command (it asks you questions), or you need to perform a repetitive operation on a one-shot basis (look for and operate on specific files in a directory).

Using simple commands like the editors is an effective use of the Shell, but less productive than joining Shell commands together to perform complex operations for you. Learning effective use of *grep, cut, paste,* and numerous other tools (as described in Chapters 2 and 3) is the essence of productivity improvement. The Shell provides a consistent environment of reusable tools that can be joined together to manipulate virtually any text into some required form. The hard part is developing the mental focus to understand this flexibility and use it in everyday activities. The Shell can quickly extract and format information or it can handle more complex, recursive procedures.

2. NONRECURSIVE PROCEDURES

It is often useful to see how other UNIX users have tackled the use of particular commands. To find out how other Shell programmers have used *while* loops, *grep* the bin directories to find the names of shells that use *while:*

```
grep -l while /bin/* /usr/bin/* /unix1/bin/* /usr/ucb/bin
```

This command will list the names of all of the files that have *while* in them. The same sort of search is useful when learning C language. (*Grep* the /usr/src/cmd directory.) Searching for examples is one of the best ways to find good examples of Shell and C-language code.

Selecting and reporting information is an excellent way to improve productivity with the Shell. Files like /etc/passwd can be inspected and printed:

```
cut -f1,5 -d: /etc/passwd : pr -o8
lja        Jay Arthur
pgm        Paula Martin
```

Finding duplicate user IDs is a snap with *cut, sort,* and *uniq:*

cut -f1 -d: /etc/passwd ¦ sort ¦ uniq -u

Using data selection commands like *grep, cut,* and *uniq* can quickly eliminate extraneous information. Reporting commands like *awk, cat, pr,* and *nroff* can then format the remaining information so that it is usable. For further information on these commands, refer to Chapters 2 and 3. Another good way to use the Shell interactively is with recursive procedures.

3.   RECURSIVE PROCEDURES

In everyday usage, you will need to perform the same operation on many files. The main Shell facilities to help you are *for, find,* and *xargs. While* and *until* are also occasionally useful. *Find* should be used to locate all the files under a specified directory and execute commands. *For* and *xargs* should be used with files in the current directory. *While* is useful when starting loops that continue while some criteria is satisfied within the loop. *Until* will execute the loop processing until a condition is met.

3.1.   *Find*

Find is invaluable when you have left a file somewhere under your login, but have no idea where. To find the file from your HOME directory type:

find . -name lostfile -print
./doc/unix/lostfile

Similarly, you can use *find* to locate files with similar names, like SCCS files:

find . -name s.* -print
./doc/sccs/book/s.chapter1
./doc/sccs/book/s.chapter2

Or for C language:

```
find . -name \*.c -print
./src/sccs/games/s.startrek.c
./src/c/header.c
```

Once you have identified that *find* is locating the proper file names,
you can execute commands on those files. However, before you execute
commands that will remove or change files, determine whether *find* is
obtaining only the file names you require. Otherwise, you could lose or
corrupt a large number of files and never know it was done. If you are
in doubt, use the *-ok* feature of *find* to check each file name before
executing the command:

```
find . -name s\* -ok rm -f { } \;
./doc/unix/book/s.chapter1? n
./doc/unix/book/s.chapter2? n
./src? n
./src/slop? y
./src/sludge? y
```

Without these checks, *find* would have removed the SCCS files containing chapters 1 and 2. Perhaps the system administrator could restore them from backup; however, recreating them would not be fun. A
simple command to remove all junk files, however, would be:

```
find . -name junk\* -exec rm -f { } \;
```

This would remove all junk files under your login directory. Similarly,
the following command would interactively remove all files not accessed for over 30 days:

```
find . -atime +30 -ok rm -f { } \;
```

Find is useful for any task that requires looking down through
directory structures, finding files, and executing commands to modify
or delete the files. It does not work well, however, when you want to

work on just the files in the current directory. For these recursive processes, you need *for* and *xargs*.

3.2. For

For lets you perform multiple operations on specified files. *Xargs,* on the other hand, can only execute one command per file. So, rather than write a separate procedure to handle the work at hand, use *for* interactively to accomplish what needs to be done. A word of caution—as the number of commands grows, there are more chances for error; it is sometimes easier to create a Shell procedure with the editor and test it than to type the *for* loop over and over again. Creating Shell procedures is described in Chapter 5.

One of the most frequent uses of the *for* loop involves editing files in the current directory to change an old word to a new one:

```
for file in chapter?
do
ed $file <<!
g/shell/s//Shell/g
w
q
!
done
```

The *for* command substitutes chapter0 through chapter9 for the variable *file* and executes the editor commands that follow.

Similarly, *for* could calculate the average length of each word in each chapter:

```
for file in chapter?
do
   totalchar = `wc -c ${file} ¦ cut -c1-7`
   totalwords = `wc -w ${file} ¦ cut -c1-7`
   average = `expr ${totalchar}/${totalwords}`
   echo ${file} ${average}
done
```

These are fairly simple examples, but they show the basic uses of *for*. When the commands within the *for* loop exceed six or seven, the chances for error increase and you should consider creating a temporary Shell procedure that can be edited and corrected. The other command for operating on files in a directory is *xargs*.

3.3. Xargs

Xargs works well on files in a directory when you only want to execute one command:

```
ls junk* ¦ xargs -i rm -f { }
```

This could have been handled more effectively as:

```
rm -f junk*
```

But remember when using *for* loops interactively, you sometimes need to create a temporary Shell procedure because the processing becomes too complex? Rather than using *for* to execute the command repetitively:

```
for file in chapter?
do
   junkproc $file
done
```

it is easier to use *xargs:*

```
ls chapter? ¦ xargs -i junkproc { }
```

Adding, getting, or creating deltas of files in SCCS is another application of *xargs*. In the following example, all the chapters can be added to SCCS with one command line:

```
ls chapter? ¦ xargs -i admin -i{ } -y"First draft" s.{ }
```

Xargs is a handy way to process many files at one time. For more complex loops, the Shell user will need *while* and *until*.

3.4.   While and Until

The *while* loop can be used interactively when you want to set a variable to a value and loop until it reaches some other value. The following simple example calculates the sine of all angles between 1° and 90°:

```
angle = 1
while [ ${angle} -le 90 ]
do
    sine = `echo "scale = 2;s(${angle})" ¦ bc -l`
    echo "Sine of ${angle} = ${sine}"
    angle = `expr ${angle} + 1`
done
```

All the values would print out on the terminal. These values could also be directed into a file or printed with *pr*.

Note that the *while* loop simplifies interactive commands that change variables other than file names. *For* and *xargs* are more effective with files.

Until could have been used in a similar fashion:

```
angle = 1
until [ ${angle} -gt 90 ]
do
    sine = `echo "scale = 2;s(${angle})" ¦ bc -l`
    echo "Sine of ${angle} = ${sine}"
    angle = `expr ${angle} + 1`
done
```

All these commands—*find, for, until, while,* and *xargs*—allow the user to execute repetitive actions on files and directories. When the user needs to interact with these commands, the process should be run in foreground. Whenever possible, however, these commands should be run in background so that the user can continue working.

4. FOREGROUND AND BACKGROUND PROCEDURES

Anytime you need immediate answers, execute Shell commands in foreground at the terminal. Because executing a command can take a long time and tie up the terminal (which you could use for other productive work), you can submit the command in background. The Shell facility to handle this is simple and easy to remember: &. The ampersand at the end of a command line tells the Shell to run the command in background. Initiating background processes can be very productive and is something everyone should learn how to do. In a previous example:

ls chapter? ¦ xargs -i junkproc { } &
2304

The Shell started up a background process and printed out the process number (2304). This number is used to reference the process. The Shell variable $! contains the number of the last background process initiated. Sometimes you will need to kill the process:

kill $!
2304 killed

or you will need to wait for it to complete:

wait 2304

Processes may also be submitted to background so that you can hang up and let the process continue (all processes are killed otherwise). The facility that allows this is called *nohup:*

nohup nightlyprocess&
15342

Nohup stands for *no hang up*. It prevents the process from terminating when a user logs off. Any output generated by the command on either stdout or stderr are placed into a file called nohup.out, which can be examined later to determine the success or failure of the processing.

To be kind to your fellow UNIX users, the priority of any background processes should be lowered to speed up terminal response time. The Shell facility to lower priorities is called *nice*. It should be used as follows:

```
nice command arg1 arg2 arg3 ... &

nohup nice command arg1 ... &
```

Note that both *find* and *xargs* lend themselves to background execution. *For, while,* and *until* are more easily initiated in foreground. But they can be executed in background using parentheses:

```
( for file in *
do
   cp $file newdir
done
)&
```

While and *until* loops can be initiated in background in the same fashion.

Some systems have a command that executes a command at a specified time. The *at* command allows a UNIX user to execute commands at night, on weekends, or on holidays without ever logging in to UNIX. It takes the following forms:

```
at 6pm nightlyprocess

at 6pm
nightlyprocess1
nightlyprocess2
cntl(d)
```

Nightlyprocess will be executed at 6 P.M. with all of the user's characteristics. The *at* command is an excellent way to off-load CPU and I/O intensive activities to the evenings or weekends. When you begin to experience degraded response time on a UNIX system, consider using *at* to reduce prime-time system load.

5. SUMMARY

Interactive Shell usage can be highly productive. It can extract and report useful information. It performs complex processes on files, directories, or whatever. Use of repetitive procedures (*find, for, until, while,* and *xargs*) and background procedures promote productivity. Processing can even be delayed into non-prime-time with commands like *at*.

Interactive Shell usage helps test prototypes of new shells. It can also be used to prototype C-language programs to eliminate bugs before coding the commands in a more efficient form.

Once you begin using the Shell interactively and discover that many interactive processes require too much typing, it is time to learn about Shell programming—putting those interactive commands into an executable and reusable file—to improve your productivity.

Complex commands should be created as Shell procedures. The development and use of Shell procedures will be described in the next chapter. Trying to perform complex activities interactively is usually frustrating, because syntax errors can easily negate all your typing. If you try an interactive command a couple of times without success, consider putting the whole thing in a Shell procedure that can be edited and corrected as errors are uncovered.

EXERCISES

1. Describe the two types of interactive Shell procedures.

2. Describe the difference between foreground and background processes. What is the Shell character that puts commands into background?

3. What command allows the Shell user to run commands in background and hangup?

4. What other ways can interactive Shell usage serve the development of Shell programs?

5. Write an interactive command to search through your directories, removing junk files. Make sure the command runs after 10 P.M. to reduce system load.

6. Write a background command to edit all of the files in the current directory, replacing the word "while" with "until."

CHAPTER

5

====================

Shell Programming

Shell programming is little more than taking the commands and control structures you have learned up to this point, combining them to form a reusable procedure, and putting them into a file that you and others can execute. Simple as that. Shell procedures provide a simple way to automate both complex and simple everyday processes.

1. WHEN TO CREATE SHELL PROGRAMS

Anytime you need to perform a complex procedure using many command lines, you need to create a Shell procedure, commonly called Shell scripts or just plain "shells" for brevity. Anytime that you uncover a way of doing something from which all users can benefit, create a Shell procedure. Anytime you find yourself entering the same simple command over and over again, create a shell. The advantage of Shell is that it has access to many small functional commands. These reusable commands can be combined to automate increasingly complex functions that you would normally do manually.

The commands supplied with UNIX are found in /bin and /usr/bin. Normally you will need to create other places to store shells for general and personal use. Shell procedures for the user community are normally stored in a separate directory like /global/bin. Commands for a particular work group or file system can be stored in their file system: /unixfs/bin. Personal procedures can be stored in $HOME/bin.

These commands can be accessed directly by modifying the PATH variable in one of the profiles—/etc/profile, .profile, .login, or .cshrc—as follows:

```
PATH = ${PATH}:/global/bin:${HOME}/bin
export PATH
```

Shell programs can then be created, tested, and stored in one of these bins for immediate access by the user.

2.   CREATING SHELL PROGRAMS

There are four basic program designs: edit, update, select, and report. Virtually all Shell programs will fall into one of these categories or they may consist of two or more of these designs.

Most Shell commands, for example, have arguments on the command line:

```
command argument1 argument2 . . .
```

So, each Shell program will need to *edit* these arguments. Other Shell programs will prompt the user for information, which must also be edited.

Still other Shell programs will *update* existing files like /etc/passwd or JCL files that are then sent to another machine via the Remote Job Entry facility. Anytime a user edits a file, he or she is updating the file.

Some Shell programs will be responsible for *selecting* and extracting information from existing files and organizing it for reporting.

Finally, other Shell programs *report* the information from selection programs or from files or directories.

The various Shell commands involved in editing, updating, selecting, and reporting information are shown in Figure 5.1. Use of these commands will be described in detail in the following sections.

Editor Commands

test   —compare two values

Update Commands

cat   —concatenate one or more files
join   —join two files together
merge   —merge two or more files together
paste   —put a file or files together
newform—convert tabs
sed   —the stream editor
tr   —a character translator

Data Selection Commands

awk   —pattern scanning and processing language
cut   —select fields in a file
grep   —select lines of a file
uniq   —select unique lines in a file

Reporting Commands

awk   —pattern scanning and processing language
cat   —display a file
nroff   —formatted output
pr   —print a file

Figure 5.1 *Edit, update, select,* and *report* commands.

In creating a Shell program, these commands are combined in various ways to accomplish the user's needs. This is the fun part. Users create procedures by entering Shell commands into a file via any of the available editors. To make the Shell file executable, change its mode:

chmod 755 shellproc

Here are a few tips for creating a shell of any complexity. First, try each command line interactively, making sure that it works as expected. The following simple example extracts a user's name from the password file by login name and reports it:

grep lja /etc/passwd ! cut -f5 -d:
Jay Arthur

If the field displacement or delimiter of the *cut* command had been wrong, I would have known it immediately. I can now include this command in a Shell procedure with faith that it works the way I want it to.

Similarly, test the shell thoroughly before subjecting the rest of the user community to it. The Shell provides a couple of interactive debugging facilities in the form of parameters (-vx).

You can execute a procedure and the Shell will display every command line as it reads it:

sh -v shellproc

Similarly, the Shell will display each command executed and the values substituted for variables:

sh -x shellproc

Several other flags can aid in debugging a new procedure (Figure 5.2). Any of these commands can be set within the procedure by use of the *set* command:

set -x

-e —exit immediately when a command returns a nonzero status
-n —read, but do not execute the commands
-t —exit after reading and executing one command
-u —treat unset variables as an error
-v —print command lines as they are read
-x —print interpreted command lines as they are executed

Figure 5.2   Shell control flags.

Any of the currently set flags are contained in the Shell variable $-.

echo $-
x

These are the basic things a user needs to know to write and test Shell procedures. To make commands reusable, however, you need to know about argument lists.

3.   ARGUMENT LISTS

When creating a Shell command, you will probably want to pass it the name of one or more files or you will need to give it some special information to affect its processing. This can be done easily with arguments to the command:

shellproc file1 file3 file5
shellproc "Jay Arthur" "lja"

The Shell recognizes each of these arguments and assigns them names that can be accessed within the program—$1, $2, $3, and so on. All the variables assigned by the Shell are shown in Figure 5.3.

shellproc file1 file3 file5
** $0 $1 $2 $3**

Bourne Shell

$CDPATH	—search path for *cd*
$HOME	—path name of the user's login directory
$MAIL	—path name of the user's mail file
$PATH	—the Shell's search path for commands
$PS1	—the primary prompt string:
	"$ " for Bourne-Shell systems
	"% " for C-Shell systems
$PS2	—the secondary prompt string: "> "
$#	—the number of positional parameters on the command line
$*n*	—argument *n* on the command line, i.e. $1
$*	—all arguments on the command line (or $@)
$-	—the flags supplied to the Shell
$?	—the return code from the previous command
$$	—the current process number
$!	—the process number of the last background command

C Shell

$argv	—all arguments on the command line
$argv[*n*]	—argument *n* on the command line
$#argv	—the number of positional parameters on the command line
$child	—the process number of the last background command
$echo	—print commands as they are executed
$history	—number of commands remembered in history
$home	—path name of the user's home directory (˜)
$ignoreeof	—ignore terminal end of file
$mail	—path name of the user's mail file
$noclobber	—do not overwrite existing files
$noglob	—inhibit file name expansion
$path	—like $PATH
$prompt	—like $PS1
$status	—like $?
$time	—maximum CPU time for commands

Figure 5.3 Shell variables.

These arguments can be changed as they are used by application of the *shift* command. *Shift* moves each argument, $1 through $#, to the left, changing the previous argument list as follows:

```
shellproc file3 file5
   $0     $1  $2
```

Shift is used with *while* loops to process arguments:

```
while [ "$1" ]
do
   process $1
   shift
done
```

This example processes each argument and then shifts the remaining arguments. When there are no more arguments, *test* will return a false value to the *while* loop and the command will exit successfully. *Shift* makes looping through arguments simple and straightforward. *Shift* is also useful for processing two or more arguments at a time:

```
while [ "$1" -a "$2" ]
do
   process $1 $2
   shift;shift
done
```

Two other Shell variables reference the arguments $1 through $#: $* and $@. These are used when one Shell procedure invokes another with the argument list. The two are almost identical except in how they pass the arguments when they are quoted—$* passes all of the arguments to the receiving command as a single argument:

```
shellproc file?

rm "$*"
is the same as
rm "file1 file3 file5"
```

$@ passes the arguments as they were originally specified so that the command can work properly:

> **rm "$@"**
> **is the same as**
> **rm "file1" "file3" "file5"**

If the executed command had been another Shell procedure instead of a *remove* command, that procedure's arguments would have varied as follows:

> **subshell "$*" (subshell "file1 file3 file5")**
> **$1 = "file1 file3 file5"**

Even if the parent shell changes into another directory containing the files file2, file4, and file6, the following substitution would have occurred using $@:

> **subshell "$@" (subshell "file1" "file3" "file5")**
> **$1 = file1**
> **$2 = file3**
> **$3 = file5**

The $* form is useful with *echo* to display all of the arguments:

> **echo "$*"**
> **file1 file3 file5**

Without the double quotes, $* and $@ are equivalent, but these two can cause confusion and problems so be careful.

Arguments to a Shell program should be edited using either the IF-THEN-ELSE construct for single arguments or the CASE construct for programs with more than one argument. Editing arguments helps improve a program's reliability.

A Shell program that expects a single argument, perhaps a file name, should test for too many arguments and for a valid file name:

```
if [ $# -eq 1 ]
then
  if [ -f $1 ]
  then
      process $1
  else
      echo "$1 is not a valid file name"
  fi
else
    echo "$0 syntax: $0 filename"
fi
```

A program with more than one argument can use the CASE construct to handle the argument edits:

```
case $# in
  0)   # oops no arguments
       echo enter argument1
       read arg1
       echo enter argument2
       read arg2
       ;;
  2)
       arg1 = $1
       arg2 = $2
       ;;
  *)
       echo "$0 syntax: $0 argument1 argument2"
       ;;
esac
```

Or a program may expect a series of flags as well as file names or whatever. Flags should be separated from the remaining arguments:

```
while [ `echo $1 ¦ cut -c1` = "-" ]
do
   case $1 in
     -a¦-b¦-c)
       flags="${flags} $1"
       ;;
     *)
       echo "$1 is not a valid flag"
       ;;
   esac
   shift
done
```

Then the tests for the remaining arguments can be performed using the CASE construct or IF-THEN-ELSE. Editing arguments is an important part of building reliable Shell programs.

4. VARIABLES

Assigning values to variables is an important feature of creating Shell procedures. Previous chapters showed how variables work with control structures (IF-THEN-ELSE, CASE, FOR, UNTIL, and WHILE). The Bourne and C Shells assign variables differently. The C Shell requires the user to *set* variables, while the Bourne Shell allows simple assignment:

        set variable = value   (C Shell)
        variable = value   (Bourne Shell)

Shell users can also create variables to improve maintainability and reusability of the procedure. A simple example involves keeping all of the boilerplate for documents—letters, memos, forms, whatever—in a unique directory. To allow for future changes in the directory name on

various systems, you might create a variable that points to the boilerplate directory:

```
docdir = "/unixfs/boilerplate"
```

Then, create a shell called *getdoc* that selectively retrieves boilerplate
from the directory:

```
docdir = "/unixfs/boilerplate"
if [ -r ${docdir}/$1 ]
then
   cp ${docdir}/$1 $2
   echo $1 boilerplate created as $2
else
   echo $1 boilerplate not found in ${docdir}
fi
```

Setting and using the variable *docdir* ensures that the command can
later be changed to point to other directories on other machines by
changing only the variable assignment, not the entire procedure. Using variables for path names is definitely desirable: they are easily
maintained and more reliable.

A common problem with new shells is that variables are referenced
before they are assigned a value. To counter the effects of this problem,
the Shell can be told to treat unset variables as fatal errors:

```
set -u
```

Or, you can specify a default value for a variable:

```
if [ -d ${docdir: = /unixfs/boilerplate} ]
```

The Shell checks to see if *docdir* has a value, if so it uses it, otherwise,
it uses /unixfs/boilerplate. Having meaningful defaults for variables
means never having to say you're sorry. They prevent improper opera-

tion of the shell. For example, suppose that you had a command that
did the following:

```
cd $temp
rm -rf *
```

If $temp has no value, the Shell will change to $HOME and remove all
of your files. This could have been avoided by:

```
cd ${temp: = /tmp}
rm -rf *
```

which would only remove those files in /tmp that belong to your user
ID.

Variables can also be set to the output of Shell commands by use of
the accent grave characters (`):

```
if cmdpath has a value of /usr/bin/nroff

dirname = `basename ${cmdpath}`
echo $dirname
/usr/bin

angle = `expr ${angle: = 0} + 1`
(add one to the variable angle)
```

The *set* command can also be used to set the command variables: $1,
$2, $3, and so on. To set these variables to all the file names in the
current directory, use the following command:

```
set - *
```

To set $1 to a new value, *set* can also be used as follows:

```
set - "new value for $1" "new value for $2" . . .
```

Variables are an important part of writing good Shell procedures. They can be assigned both string and numeric values from any source including the output of other Shell commands. Put them all together with arguments, commands, and control structures, and you have the ability to manipulate files into any required format.

5. BUILT-IN COMMANDS

The Shell uses certain commands that are built in. The Bourne and C Shell built-in commands are shown in Figures 5.4 and 5.5. The com-

Bourne Shell

break   —leave a *for, until,* or *while* loop
continue—continue next execution of a loop
cd   —change directory
eval   —evaluate and execute a command
exec   —execute in place of the current command
exit   —leave the shell
export   —make variables available to subsequent commands
newgrp   —change groups
read   —read a line from standard input
readonly—same as export, except variables cannot be modified
set   —set Shell flags and arguments
shift   —shift arguments from $2 to $1
test   —see the *test* command
times   —print user and system times
trap   —see the *trap* command
ulimit   —limit file sizes
umask   —see the *umask* command
wait   —wait on a process to complete

Figure 5.4   Bourne-Shell built-in commands.

C Shell

alias	—create an alias
alloc	—show core allocation
break	—leave a *for*, *until*, or *while* loop
breaksw	—leave a *switch* statement
cd	—change directory (also chdir)
continue	—continue next execution of a loop
echo	—see the *echo* command
exec	—execute in place of the current command
exit	—leave the shell
glob	—like the *echo* command but with no escapes "\"
goto	—go to a label in the shell
history	—display history event list
logout	—terminate the login shell
nice	—execute command at a lower priority
nohup	—ignore hangups
onintr	—handle interrupts
set	—set Shell flags, arguments, and variables
setenv	—set environment variables
shift	—shift arguments from $2 to $1
source	—get shell commands from a source file
time	—print user and system times
umask	—see the *umask* command
unalias	—delete an alias
unset	—delete a variable
wait	—wait for a process to complete
@	—set a variable to an expression
*=, +=, -=, /=, etc.	—same as C language
++, --	—same as C language

Figure 5.5 C-Shell built-in commands.

mands *break, cd, exit, export, set, shift,* and *test* have been demonstrated in prior examples. Of equal importance are the *eval, exec, read, trap,* and *wait* commands.

The *eval* command lets the user build command strings and then evaluate and execute them as input to the Shell. For example, a complicated shell command might have to determine the proper input and output filters for a given command. Rather than execute the command many different ways, the shell could create a variable containing the correct input filters and one containing the proper output filters. The complete command could be evaluated and executed as follows:

```
inputfilter = "cmd1 ¦ cmd2"
outputfilter = "cmd3 ¦ cmd4"
eval "$inputfilter ¦ command ¦ $outputfilter"
```

which would be the equivalent of executing the commands:

```
cmd1 ¦ cmd2 ¦ command ¦ cmd3 ¦ cmd4
```

An example of this nature is developed in Chapter 9. Using *eval* can reduce the complexity and improve the maintainability of many Shell programs.

The *exec* command will execute a command *in place of* the current command without creating a new process. This is occasionally useful if control need never return to the parent shell. A more useful form reads a file as input and executes the commands as if they were part of the current shell program:

```
. command          (Bourne Shell)
source command     (C Shell)
```

The Shell code in *command* is reusable by any command that needs it. Reusability, in turn, can reduce maintenance costs—rather than fix 10 versions of the same code, only one command need be changed.

The *read* command gets a line from standard input. In most cases, stdin will be a terminal. In most Shell programs, if the user does not enter the correct number of arguments, it is better to ask for them than to exit and demand that they be entered on the command line. A combination of *echo* and *read* handles the job nicely:

```
if [ $# -eq 0 ]
then
    echo "Enter filename"
    read filename
else
    filename = $1
fi
```

Read can also get a line of input from a file or pipe used as standard input:

```
shellcommand < file
command ! shellcommand

#shellcommand
while read inputline
do
    process inputline
done
```

This could also be handled by the *line* command:

```
while inputline = `line`
etc.
```

The *read* command is a handy built-in function to get information from the standard input and assign the result to a variable that can then be handled like any other.

The *trap* command handles interrupts like hang up (1), delete (2), and break (3). It is mainly useful for cleaning up after a command is interrupted or for ignoring interrupts entirely. The following commands alternately clean up and ignore the interrupts:

```
trap "rm /tmp/tmp$$; exit 1" 1 2 3
trap "" 1 2 3
```

Trap is useful for graceful tolerance of all kinds of faults and interruptions. It helps improve a program's reliability.

The *wait* command, as its name implies, waits for a background processes to complete before continuing. A Shell program might start a background process, do some other processing, and then have to wait for the background process (or processes) to complete before continuing. *Wait* is a patient command:

```
command& # put the command in background

   other
   shell
   commands

wait $-   # wait for the last background command to finish
wait      # wait for all background commands to finish
   continue processing
```

Wait, like the rest of these built-in commands, meets special needs of the Shell programmer. They help make it simple to build useful Shell procedures.

6. SHELL PROCEDURES

To illustrate the prior facilities and concepts, let's develop a few shells, ranging from simple to complex.

The *who* command tells who is logged onto the system at any time, but it only tells the person's login ID, not his or her name. This information is in the password file, but not in a form that can be used easily. Let's develop a command, called *whois,* to extract the user from the password file and print only the relevant information.

First, we need to extract the user ID from the /etc/passwd file and then extract only the person's name. *Whois* will have the following form:

```
# whois userid
if [ $# -eq 0 ]
then
# no user ids supplied
   echo "Enter userid"
   read userid
   grep $userid /etc/passwd : cut -f5 -d:
else
   grep $1 /etc/passwd : cut -f5 -d:
fi

whois lja
Jay Arthur
```

To make this command work on more than one userid, it could be modified as follows:

```
# whois userid(s)
if [ $# -eq 0 ]
then
# no user ids supplied
   echo "Enter userid"
   read userid
   grep $userid /etc/passwd : cut -f5 -d:
else
   while [ "$1" ]
   do
      grep $1 /etc/passwd : cut -f5 -d:
      shift
   done
fi
```

The command could be made more efficient by using *egrep* and pasting all of the arguments together as follows:

```
# whois userid(s)
if [ $# -eq 0 ]
then
# no user ids supplied
   echo "Enter userid"
   read userid
   grep $userid /etc/passwd ¦ cut -f5 -d:
else
   grepstr = $1
   shift
   while [ "$1" ]
   do
      grepstr = "${grepstr}\\¦$1"
      shift
   done
   egrep ${grepstr} /etc/passwd ¦ cut -f5 -d:
fi
```

Another simple Shell procedure might need to look through all directories under the current one and execute commands entered by the user. This command should also trap interrupts and allow processing to continue:

```
# dirsearch [ directory_name ]
# search the specified directory for other directories
# in each one, prompt the user for commands to be executed.
if [ -d "$1" ]
then
   cd $1                              # change directory to $1
else
   dir = `pwd`                        # dir = current directory
```

```
        for file in *                    # all files in directory
        do
          if [ -d $file ]                # directory ?
          then
            cd ${dir}/${file}
            while echo "${file} ?"
              trap "exit 0" 1 2 3
              read cmd                    # read command
            do
              trap "" 1 2 3
              eval $cmd                   # execute command
            done
            cd ..
          fi
        done
    fi
```

Another simple but useful command displays information on the screen a page at a time. Using *cat* to display a file often causes the important information to disappear before the user can hit the no scroll key. A simple command to display pages on 25 line terminals is:

```
pr -p -t -123 filename      # pause every 23 lines
```

But on other occasions, it would be nice to page through the output of another command:

```
nroff -cm document ! pr -p -t -123
```

These can be combined into a single Shell that handles whatever it is given:

```
# page [files]
case $# in
  0)
        # if the terminal is standard input and
        # there are no arguments
```

```
         # prompt for a file name
         if [ -t 0 ] # standard input is a terminal
         then
             echo "What file?"
             read filename
             pr -p -t -123 ${filename: = /dev/null}
         else      # read from standard input
             pr -p -t -123 <&0
         fi
         ;;
     *)
         while [ "$1" ]
         do
             echo "Printing $1"
             pr -p -t -123 $1
             shift
         done
         ;;
     esac
```

Another example involves a directory that contains files or commands spooled by another command. If the first line of each file contains a header line with the user's ID and other information, the user can check the status of those jobs as follows:

```
#status
spooldir = /usr/spool/whatever
cd ${spooldir}
( for files in *               # all files in spool directory
  do
     line < ${files}           # read first line
  done
) | grep ${LOGNAME}            # grep userid from first lines
```

In this example, *line* will extract the first line of each file in /usr/spool/whatever. Because the *for* loop is enclosed in parentheses, all the output from each of the *line* commands is placed on stdout. Instead of many separate streams of information, the Shell combines the output of each of the *line* commands into a single stream that can be piped into *grep*. *Grep* then looks through the stream for header lines that match the user's login name, ${LOGNAME}.

Another simple need of a Shell user would be to execute a series of commands, but execute them at intervals so that the system's users would notice little degradation. The command to read a command from an input file and execute it at 15-minute intervals would look like this:

```
# nohup today < commandfile&
while cmd = `line`          # get line from commandfile
      test -n "${cmd}"
do
      eval ${cmd}            # execute command
      sleep 900             # sleep 15 minutes
done
```

The possibilities for creating useful commands seems endless. It requires some ingenuity to pick the best combination of commands, pipes, redirection, and Shell constructs to build a new shell, but with a little experience it is easy. One of the best ways to get new ideas is

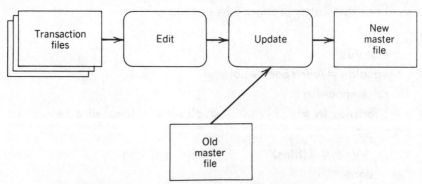

Figure 5.6 Edit and update program design.

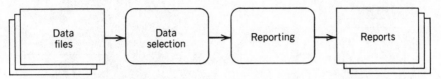

Figure 5.7 Data selection and report program design.

to study the shells that come with UNIX: those in /bin, /usr/bin, and /usr/ucb/bin.

As previously mentioned, Shell programs come in four common flavors: edit, update, select, and report. The edit and update processes *create* information. Data from the terminal or files should be edited and then used as input to the update process, as shown in Figure 5.6. The select and report processes gather information and present it in a usable manner. Information is selected by Shell commands and then reported with others, as shown in Figure 5.7.

This section has introduced some of the basic ways to use Shell commands, and the following sections will delve into each of these four basic program designs and ways to implement each in Shell Language.

7. EDIT

Getting valid file or directory names, correct string and numeric variables, and so on is essential to having a Shell program execute correctly and reliably. To ensure that all variables, files, and special files are valid requires an edit test. Is the file name correct and is the file readable? Writable? Executable? Is the name a directory, block special, or character special file? Is a variable equal to a specified value or other variable? Each of these questions is answered by editing the data within the Shell procedure (Figure 5.8). The primary command for editing data is *test*.

Test combined with the *if-then-else* handles most edits on arguments or data in a Shell program. The *case* statement handles the rest of the edits normally required.

Arguments to the Shell program are normally entered by humans and as such, are most prone to error. These should always be edited for validity before using them in processing. The Shell variables that hold

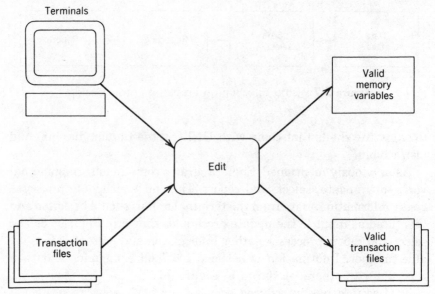

Figure 5.8 Interactive and sequential edit program design.

each of the program's arguments are $0, $1, $2, and so on. These arguments come in two forms: flags and data (numbers, text, or file names).

flags	text	numbers	files
command -flag1 -flag2 ...	"report header"	123	file1 file2 ...

Flags (in the form -s, -l66, etc.) pass user-specified controls into the Shell program. Flags may tell the program to suppress printing errors (-s) or that the length of the page is 66 (-l66) or any number of other ways to change the natural function of the program. Performing edit checks on flags is easiest with the CASE construct:

```
while ( `echo $1 ; cut -c1` = "-" )          # arg $1 is a flag
do
  case $1
    -)                                        # use stdin as input
        stdinflag = 1
      ;;
```

```
        -d)                                  # suppress data output
            dataflag = 1
            ;;
        -l*)                                 # get line length
            linelength = `echo $1 ; cut -c3-`
            ;;
        -s)                                  # suppress error messages
            suppressflag = 1
            ;;
        *)
            echo "Incorrect flag $1"
            ;;
    esac
    shift
done
```

These values can be tested later to determine the correct processing:

```
if [ "${stdinflag}" ]        # if stdinflag is set use standard input
then
  pr <&0
else                         # print the first file
  pr $1
fi
```

The other arguments to a Shell program are typically files, directories, special files, or an occasional text or numeric value for inclusion
in printed material. Each of these values should be edited for validity
before using them in a Shell procedure. *Test* handles these validations
easily:

```
if [ -f $1 -a -r $1 ]        # if $1 is a readable file
if [ -f $1 -a -s $1 ]        # if $1 is a nonzero length file
if [ -d $1 -a -x $1 ]        # if $1 is an executable directory
if [ "$1" ]                  # if $1 has a value
```

```
if [ "$1" = "lja" ]                 # if $1 is equal to my login name
if [ "$1" = "${variable}" ]         # if $1 is equal to some variable
if [ "$1" -lt 100 ]                 # if $1 is a valid year 00–99
# valid month
if [ ${month} -ge 1 -a ${month} -le 12 ]
if [ -t 0 ]                         # stdin is a terminal
```

Test allows the user to test for the existence and permissions on a file or directory. It can also handle simple comparisons and range tests that are required when editing input arguments or data. All the tests and comparisons allowed by *test* are shown in Figure 3.1.

Another common editing requirement involves interactive commands. These commands prompt the user with questions and then read the answers, edit them for validity, and take some action. The following example prompts the user with file names for removal:

```
echo "Answer y/n to the following"
for file in *
do
    if [ -f ${file} -a -w ${file} ]      # removable file?
    then
        echo "Remove ${file}?"
        read answer
        if [ "${answer}" = "y" ]         # Yes?
        then
            rm ${file}
        fi                               # else don't remove
    fi
done
```

Even arguments on command lines, like the preceding *for* loop, can be edited before processing is allowed. In this example, the Shell program will test ${file} to ensure that it is a file and is writable before prompting the user. These edits prevent the Shell from operating with incorrect or improper data.

The *if-then-else, test,* and *case* statements are the primary means of editing data in a Shell before using the information. Editing ensures that the data is not garbage, but usable information. The next section will describe how to use Shell commands to update files with the data validated in the editing process.

8. UPDATE

Updating a file means adding, changing, or deleting data from it. The design of a simple sequential update program is shown in Figure 5.9. There are one or more possible transaction files that affect the original or master file. The master (or old) file is used as input and a new file is created as output. Any errors are directed onto stderr.

The Shell commands that handle most of the common updates to UNIX files are *cat, join, merge, newform, paste, sed,* and *tr.* The UNIX editors also update files, but they do so manually rather than mechanically. This section will deal with the automated forms of file update.

The simplest update program is *cat,* which can create new files, concatenate several files into one new file, or append one file to an existing file. Each of these forms of update is shown in the following examples:

```
cat > file              # enter data from the terminal
cat file1 file2 > file3   # create a new file from two
cat file3 >> file4        # append file3 to file4
```

In each of these examples, *cat* adds data to a new or existing file.

Cat works well for creating or adding lines to a file as long as there is no concern about the order of that information. When the information should be in order, however, either *sort* or *merge* (sort -m) serve as better update programs.

Sort can put one or more files into a specified order. This form of update is best used on unsorted files:

```
sort file1 file2 > file3
```

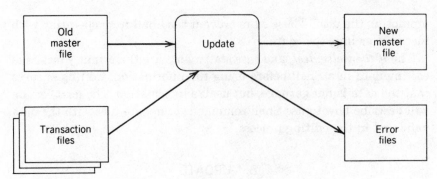

Figure 5.9 Update program design.

When the transaction and master files are already in order, however, it is more efficient to simply merge them:

sort -m master trans1 trans2 > newmaster

A simple example involves listing two directories and merging the files found:

ls /bin > binlist
ls /usr/bin > usrbinlist
sort -m binlist usrbinlist > combinedlist

When updating files in this way, duplicate entries may cause problems. There should not be two records exactly the same in the resulting new master file. To eliminate duplicates, the output can be passed through *uniq:*

sort -m master trans1 ¦ uniq > newmaster
sort -mu master trans1 > newmaster

Each of these examples using *sort* assumed that the first field in each file was the sort key. The use of other keys which can be specified with positional parameters is described in Chapter 2.

Another command that updates by matching on specific fields is *join. Join,* however, does not merge lines. When it finds matching records in the two input files, it creates a single output record containing any or all of the fields in both records. Imagine two files with the following lines in each file:

File1	File2
Arthur:555-1234	Arthur:123 Main:Denver:CO:80202
Martin:555-2345	Martin:245 Juniper:Denver:CO:80202
Smith:555-3456	

The command, *join -t: file1 file2*, will produce:

Arthur:555-1234:123 Main:Denver:CO:80202
Martin:555-2345:245 Juniper:Denver:CO:80202

Only the matched lines are joined to create an output line. To generate an output line for all lines in file1, replacing empty fields by "NA," the command could be changed to:

join -a1 -e "NA" -t: file1 file2

Arthur:555-1234:123 Main:Denver:CO:80202
Martin:555-2345:245 Juniper:Denver:CO:80202
Smith:555-3456:NA:NA:NA:NA

To get just the name, phone number, and zip code from these files, *join* would be invoked as:

join -a1 -e "NA" -o 1.1,1.2,2.5 -t: file1 file2

Arthur:555-1234:80202
Martin:555-2345:80202
Smith:555-3456:NA

The -o option specifies that only fields one and two (1.1 and 1.2) in file1 and the fifth field of file2 (2.5) should be output.

Join as shown in these examples, updates files by adding fields or creating whole new files with subsets of the fields in the original files. It is another tool in the arsenal for updating files.

Paste works similar to *join* by putting two files together regardless of their order:

paste -d: file1 file2

Arthur:555-1234:Arthur:123 Main:Denver:CO:80202
Martin:555-2345:Martin:245 Juniper:Denver:CO:80202
Smith:555-3456:::::

Paste, in this form, gives the user another kind of update capability. It is more primitive than either *join* or *merge*, but it often serves a useful purpose in Shell programming.

The commands that actually change information within a file are *newform, sed,* and *tr. Newform* changes the tab settings within the file. It is described in Chapter 2. *Tr* translates characters within a file. To change the text in the file to uppercase would require the following command:

tr "[a-z]" "[A-Z]" < file2

ARTHUR:123 MAIN:DENVER:CO:80202
MARTIN:245 JUNIPER:DENVER:CO:80202

Sed lets the user update fields within the file. For example, assume that everyone moved to San Francisco, California. *Sed* could handle all updates as follows:

sed -e "s/Denver/San Francisco/" -e "s/CO/CA/" file2

Arthur:123 Main:San Francisco:CA:80202
Martin:245 Juniper:San Francisco:CA:80202

Or the edit commands, including the zip code change, could have been placed in a file called *citystate:*

```
s/Denver/San Francisco/
s/CO/CA/
s/80202/74539/
```

Then, *sed* could be invoked as follows:

```
sed -f citystate file2
```

To delete information from files, *sed* can selectively delete lines or
parts of fields from files. To delete all of the records for people on
Juniper Street and the word "Denver" from file2, the following command would be required:

```
sed -e "/Juniper/d" -e "s/Denver//g" file2
```

```
Arthur:123 Main::CO:80202
```

"/Juniper/d" is a line editor command to delete lines containing the
word "Juniper." "s/Denver//g" is the line editor command to substitute
nothing (//) for each occurrence of the word "Denver." Using these
editor commands, *sed* acts like a program that updates fields or deletes
lines.

Each of the commands presented in this section serves a specific
purpose when updating UNIX files. Once the files have been updated
and put in correct order, the data will need to be retrieved and printed.
The commands to do so will be described in the next two sections: Data
Selection and Reporting.

9.   DATA SELECTION

Selecting information from files can be handled in a number of ways
with the Shell. Information can be selected line by line, field by field, or
both. A typical data selection program design is shown in Figure 5.10.

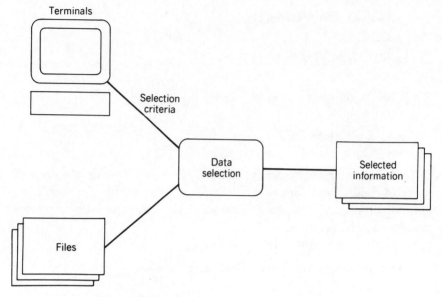

Figure 5.10 Data selection program design.

The primary commands that perform data selection are *awk, cut, grep,* and *uniq.*

Uniq is perhaps the simplest. It works on a line-by-line basis, eliminating duplicate lines or every line *except* for the duplicate lines. *Uniq* assumes that its input is sorted. Given the following sorted file called *names,* note how *uniq* selects the various lines in the file:

    Arthur
    Martin
    Martin
    Smith

uniq names	**uniq -u names**	**uniq -d names**
Arthur	**Arthur**	**Martin**
Martin	**Smith**	
Smith		

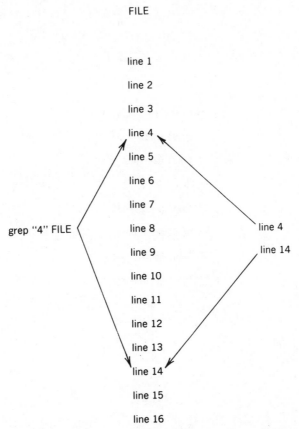

Figure 5.11   Using *grep* to select information by field.

The first example removes the duplicate name "Martin." The second eliminates "Martin" entirely. The final example eliminates all names except "Martin." *Uniq* provides an efficient tool for selecting information from files that contain duplicate lines.

Grep also operates on a line-by-line basis. It looks through a file for lines that contain the regular expression specified. Any matching records are selected. The extended *grep* (*egrep*) and fast *grep* (*fgrep*) commands provide for selecting on more than one regular expression at a time or by matching entire lines. Figure 5.11 shows how *grep* selects information from files.

cut -f2 −d: FILE

FILE

field1:field2:field3

field1:field2:field3

field1:field2:field3

field1:field2:field3

field1:field2:field3

field1:field2:field3

field1:field2:field3

field1:field2:field3

field2

field2

field2

field2

field2

field2

field2

field2

Figure 5.12 Using *cut* to select information by field.

Given the following file, *grep* and its cousins can extract information
and place it on stdout:

> Arthur Denver CO
> Martin Denver CO
> Smith Colorado Springs CO
>
> grep "Denver" file
>
> Arthur Denver CO
> Martin Denver CO
>
> egrep Martin\:Smith file
>
> Martin Denver CO
> Smith Colorado Springs CO
>
> fgrep "Martin Denver CO" file
>
> Martin Denver CO

To select information on a field-by-field basis requires the use of *cut*
(Figure 5.12). *Cut* can select fields from a file based on the character
positions of those fields or by the delimiters that separate the fields.
The most common example of selecting fields by delimiter uses the
/etc/passwd file. The fields selected are the user's login name (-f1) and
their name (-f5):

> cut -d: -f1,5 /etc/passwd
>
> ets:Ted Smith
> lja:Jay Arthur
> pgm:Paula Martin

Fields can also be selected by their character position within a file.
Consider a long listing of a directory:

ls -l

drwxrwx ----	3 lja	adm	992 Dec	1 05:39 bin
drwx ---------	28 lja	adm	496 Dec	4 12:28 doc
drwxr-x -----	2 lja	adm	192 Sep	5 17:55 jcl
drwx ---------	2 lja	adm	816 Sep	5 16:15 job
drwxrwxrwx	2 lja	adm	3760 Dec	3 09:37 rje
drwxrwxrwx	32 lja	adm	1008 Dec	3 18:22 src

Fields can be selected by column:

cut -c16-24,55-

lja	bin
lja	doc
lja	jcl
lja	job
lja	rje
lja	src

In this example, *cut* selected only the information contained in columns 16–24 and 55 through the end of each line. In both of these examples, *cut* shows its ability to select specific information for future reporting. In this particular example, the output was suitable for human consumption.

Grep and *cut* can be combined to extract information line by line and field by field. The output of *grep* can be piped into *cut*. In the following example, the commands extract all the users in the "unix1" file system from the /etc/passwd file and then extract the user's name from the file:

grep "unix1" /etc/passwd ¦ cut -f5 -d:

Jay Arthur
Paula Martin

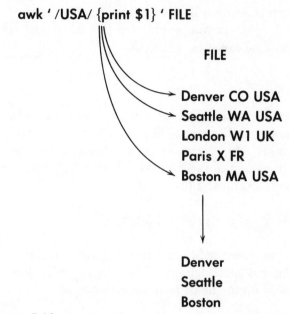

Figure 5.13   Using *awk* to select and report information.

Another command, called *awk*, handles both line-by-line and field-by-field data selection (Figure 5.13). *Awk* can do both at once. Why not use it all of the time instead of *grep* and *cut*? Well, *awk* has to interpret a data selection and reporting program, and then process the file. For less sophisticated processing, *grep* and *cut* are optimized to do their job more efficiently. When more exotic data selection criteria are applied to a file, however, *awk* gives the user more flexibility.

For example, the previous example could have been written in *awk* as:

```
BEGIN { FS = ":" } # field separator is a colon
/unix1/ { print $5 }
```

This program sets the file separator (FS) to a colon (:) and then in the processing section looks for all records that match the string "unix1" and prints the fifth field in the records matched. Assuming that this *awk* program was stored in a file called *passwd_select,* the command could be executed as follows:

awk -f passwd_select /etc/passwd

As data selection criteria become more complex, *awk* can greatly enhance the user's ability to get at the information stored in files. In another example using the previous long listing of a directory, *awk* can extract the lines containing files last updated in September and print just the owner, group, and file name as follows:

ls -l ¦ awk '/Sep/ { print $3, $4, $9 }'

Without a specified field separator (FS), *awk* assumes that white space (blanks and tabs) delimit fields. The following lines show how *awk* would pick up the fields from each record:

$1	$2	$3	$4	$5	$6	$7	$8	$9
drwxr-x---	2	lja	adm	192	Sep	5	17:55	jcl

The resulting output would be:

lja adm jcl
lja adm job

Awk can also select information from fields within each line. In the following *awk* program, the hours and minutes are selected from a long directory listing:

```
split( $8, hourmin, ":" )
print hourmin[0];     # print the hours first
print hourmin[1];     # print the minutes next
```

This particular example splits the hours and minutes field ($8) by use of the delimiter (":") and places the two resulting numbers into the two-dimensional array hourmin. The following two statements print the hours (hourmin[0]) on one line and the minutes (hourmin[1]) on the next. This would produce two lines for each line from the long listing. The same processing using *grep* and *cut* would have been more complex. *Awk* handles the processing more clearly.

As shown in these examples, *awk* can handle the functions of *grep, cut, paste,* and *pr. Awk* also has the basic control structures *if-then-else, for,* and *while.* Almost any data selection or reporting need can be programmed in *awk.*

Once the information has been extracted from a file using *grep, cut, sed,* or *awk,* it needs to be reported in ways that humans can best use. Many Shell commands support clear concise reports. Section 10 will describe these commands in detail.

10.   REPORTING

The design of a typical report program is shown in Figure 5.14. Notice that it is very similar to the design of a typical UNIX command, using stdin and stdout. Each of the standard Shell commands produces reportlike output that is fairly legible. The *cat* command will reproduce files on either the terminal screen or a printer. Commands like *ls* and *who* generate readable listings. But when data selection commands like *grep, cut,* and *awk* have been used on files, often a more specific reporting mechanism is required to make the output readable.

The two major facilities for reporting information are *pr* and *awk. Pr* produces paginated reports that fit the printed page or a terminal screen. *Awk* can handle more exacting report specifications.

Using *pr* with terminal screens was described in Section 6—Shell Procedures. The developed command was called *page.*

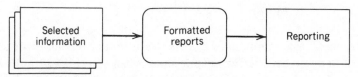

Figure 5.14   Report generation program design.

Printing files or selected information on a printer is more useful
when the output is offset by eight characters:

pr -o8 file

Files with field delimiters like the colon (:) can be printed more
legibly with *pr:*

cut -f1,5 -d: /etc/passwd ! pr -e: -o8

> lja   Jay Arthur
> pgm   Paula Martin

Printing these two fields in reverse order would have been much
more difficult. You should try using *cut, paste,* and *pr* to print the fields
in the reverse order. It is easier to use *awk* when manipulating fields.
The *awk* program to reverse these fields and print them would be:

awk -F: '{ print $5, $1 }' /etc/passwd

Jay Arthur lja
Paula Martin pgm

To obtain a more readable version of this report, the program could
have used *printf,* and *awk* function that is exactly like the C-language
function by the same name:

BEGIN { FS = ":" }
{ printf "\t%-15s %s\n", $5, $1 }

> Jay Arthur   lja
> Paula Martin   pgm

The *printf* statement uses a format statement (enclosed in double
quotes) to describe how the output should look. In this example, there
is a tab character, a left-aligned string of length 15 (%-15s), another
(left-aligned) string (%s), and a newline character (\n). The first and

printf " format string ", arg1, arg2, arg3, ...

Type	Format	Value
decimal	%d	15
	%.4d	0015
float	%f	123.45600
	%3.2f	123.45
character	%c	'a'
string	%s	filename
	%10s	filename (right aligned)
	%-10s	filename (left aligned)

Figure 5.15 Output format specifications for awk.

fifth fields of the /etc/passwd file are formatted in reverse order using this format specification. More complex formatting operations can be handled with *awk* and *printf*. The most commonly used formatting options for *printf* are shown in Figure 5.15.

Awk is the best Shell tool for formatting detailed reports. For more information, see the various *awk* references in the bibliography.

11. SUMMARY

Shell procedures are simple to create—put a group of commands into a file and make the file executable. Shells should be created anytime it requires too much typing to enter the commands interactively or when the series of commands can be reused by many users.

Arguments, variables, pipes, input/output redirection, Shell control constructs, and all the existing commands are available for command construction. Because of the simplicity of command interfaces, one Shell program can interface with another Shell or a native command. Increasingly complex processes can be automated with groups of Shell programs. Whole systems can be built with Shell. Once the system has been shaken out and the user's requests for changes decrease, Shell programs can be rewritten in C language for efficiency. But writing in C language before all the requirements are known is often a burden. Use Shell to design a working model of what is needed. If it becomes too complex or slow, it can be rewritten in C. Otherwise, Shell is more maintainable, and the Shell programming language should be used.

Most Shell programs fall into one or more of the common categories: edit, update, select, and report. Each of the available UNIX commands in some way supports these program designs. The Shell can edit, update, select data, and report results using the various commands that support each of these types of program designs. Any Shell user should become familiar with the various capabilities of these commands.

Subsequent chapters will give more examples of Shell programs. Chapter 8 will explore advanced Shell programming concepts. Examples are the best way to learn Shell concepts. Then, trying your own shells will help cement an understanding of how Shell programming can automate much of the routine daily work of a programmer, analyst, or manager.

EXERCISES

1. When should you use the Shell to create programs?

2. What are the four basic program designs most often created in Shell?

3. Which Shell commands are used in each of the basic program designs?

4. How are Shell programs created? How are they made executable?

5. What Shell options allow for "verbose" testing of Shell programs?

6. Which Shell variables contain the arguments to a Shell?

7. What Shell command changes the values of these variables?

8. Describe the difference between $* and $@.

9. What are the Shell *built-in* commands?

10. Write a Shell program to test for three arguments: arg1, arg2, and arg3. If they are not present, prompt the user to enter them.

11. Write a Shell program to test for arguments of the form: -c, -d, -e, and so forth. Set arguments by the same names (c, d, e) to TRUE (1) or FALSE (0) depending on whether the argument exists on the command line.

12. Write a Shell program to loop through the arguments on the command line and process them if they are files.

13. Combine Exercises 11 and 12 into one program to loop through the dashed arguments like -c, shifting the Shell variables, and then loop through the remaining arguments processing them if they are files.

14. Expand Exercise 13 to prompt the user for file names if none are specified. Multiple file names are possible, so loop through the prompt sequence until the user enters a return without any file name.

15. Describe and write a program to use accent grave characters (`) to assign values to variables in a Shell program.

CHAPTER

6

Microcomputer Shell Programming

UNIX is possibly the only operating system to be ported from minicomputers into microprocessors, mainframes, and supercomputer systems. One of the first successful ports to microcomputers was XENIX, Microsoft's port of UNIX Version 7. When IBM brought out its first personal computer, Microsoft handled the operating system—MS-DOS. MS-DOS evolved from a simple microcomputer operating system into progressively more UNIX-like versions. Version 2.0 had a hierarchical file system, paths, and input/output redirection. Future versions will have more UNIX-like facilities, including multitasking and multi-user capabilities.

Along with MS-DOS 2.0, IBM introduced the next version of its personal computer—the PC/XT, which had a UNIX Version 3.0 operating system available called PC/IX. Shortly thereafter, the newly divested AT&T introduced a series of microcomputers that ran UNIX

System V. IBM then introduced the PC/AT that ran XENIX, Microsoft's port of UNIX. At this writing, there are rumors of IBM unleashing a System V UNIX microcomputer. Other versions of UNIX— VENIX, Coherent, and Idris—also expand the microcomputer horizons of UNIX. But it is ultimately AT&T and IBM that will determine the future of microcomputer UNIX. With their support, microcomputer UNIX will become a reality and Shell programming is an important part of that success.

Again, Shell programming is an important part of productivity in a microcomputer environment. Each of the forthcoming UNIX operating systems for personal computers will use the Shell. MS-DOS, PC/IX, XENIX, and UNIX will each provide users with opportunities. The Shell is the key to unlocking those doors.

1. MS-DOS

Microsoft's Disk Operating System was the first overwhelmingly successful 16-bit personal computer operating system. It was fairly simple, allowing users to operate one program at a time on two floppy disk drives.

Version 2.0 of MS-DOS followed the concepts of UNIX quite closely. Command names were made more meaningful (e.g., *cp* became *copy*). Path names were specified with the backslash (\) instead of the slash (/). Standard output could be redirected into files. Argument lists could be addressed by thinly veiled Shell variables such as %1 and %2. MS-DOS became nothing more than a simplified single-user version of UNIX for the Personal Computer.

In all versions of MS-DOS, PC users could put commands into files and execute them. These command files are similar to Shell procedures. The only difference is that they all have a suffix to the command name (.bat), which stands for batch. Every MS-DOS user should have some concept of how the Shell works and how it can help get work done more easily. The following example will compile and link a C-language program using the Lattice C compiler and the Microsoft linkage editor:

```
mc1 %1.c
mc2 %1
link cs + %1,%1,,mcs
```

To compile and link a program named prog.c, the DOS user would enter the following command:

cc prog

The *cc.bat* command would substitute "prog" for every occurrence of %1, causing the compiler to generate an object file called prog.obj and an executable file called prog.exe. The *cc.bat* command acts like any Shell command, substituting arguments and executing commands under DOS instead of under UNIX.

The MS-DOS Shell offers two control structures: the IF-THEN-ELSE and the FOR loop. Each mimics its Bourne Shell counterpart. The following examples compare the MS-DOS and Bourne Shell commands for testing return codes, testing for files, comparing values, and looping through a select group of files using metacharacters for file name expansion:

MS-DOS	Bourne Shell
if errorlevel 0 echo No Error	if [$? -eq 0] then echo No Error fi
if exist file.txt print file.txt	if [-r file.txt] then pr file.txt fi
if %1 = = test echo Valid Input	if [$1 = "test"] then echo Valid Input fi
for %%v in (*.txt) do print %%v	for var in *.txt do pr $var done

Please note that you should use %%v in .bat files and %v interactively. Also, in MS-DOS version 2.11, the *for* command cannot execute another .bat file repetitively. Only the basic MS-DOS commands
can be executed repetitively.

MS-DOS can simulate the WHILE and UNTIL control structures of
the Shell using *goto* and *shift*. *Shift* works just like the Shell command
to shift from one argument to the next. *Goto* is a MS-DOS command
that branches to labels. However, *:while* is a label. The following examples compare the MS-DOS and Bourne Shell WHILE constructs:

```
:while                        while [ "$1" ]
   echo %1                    do
   shift                         echo $1; shift
   if exist %1 goto while      done
```

These commands will echo each argument input on the command
line. Then the first argument is shifted off and the second argument
becomes the first argument. The two commands then test for an argument and if there is one, they continue to loop or they exit. The MS-
DOS loop continues by going to the label *while*. The Bourne Shell loop
continues by nature of its design. The UNTIL control structure can be
duplicated in MS-DOS as follows:

```
:until                              until [ ! "$1" ]
   if not exist %1 goto endloop     do
   echo %1                             echo $1
   shift                               shift
   goto until                       done
:endloop
```

Other useful MS-DOS commands include *cls, echo, pause,* and *rem.*
Cls clears the screen so that output will begin at the top of the screen
instead of scrolling up from wherever the cursor happens to be. *Echo*
works like *set.* In normal mode, MS-DOS echos each batch command
line as it executes. Once a command has been tested, this is unnecessary. Thus *echo* can turn off this mode of operation. It should be used in

conjunction with *cls* to clear the screen (because the *echo off* command is always displayed):

```
echo off
cls
batch commands
```

The *pause* command displays a message (Strike any key when ready. . .) and waits for input. This allows the batch file developer to pause after displaying messages, before clearing the screen, and to wait for some user action (like putting a new floppy disk in drive A). A similar action is possible in Shell:

```
pause                          echo "Hit return when ready"
                               read arg
```

The *rem* (remarks) command acts similarly to *echo* except that its remark will be displayed only if *echo* is on. It is useful for putting execution comments into a batch program:

```
rem Printing file %1
```

MS-DOS also provides a hook to nonstandard command interpreters. A user can specify his or her own interpreter by using the *shell* command in the *config.sys* file. Whenever the system is brought up, MS-DOS reads the *config.sys* file to determine special configurations for the machine. The following line would load a special command interpreter (\unix\shell) installed on a user's personal computer:

```
shell = c:\unix\shell.com
```

MS-DOS can imitate most Shell control structures and handle most of the needs of a personal computer user. Batch files can work just like Shell programs to automate complex and repetitive activities.

Since MS-DOS seems to be evolving toward XENIX or System V— Microsoft's ports of UNIX to 8- and 16-bit processors, it is logical to assume that ultimately most business-oriented personal computers will run some form of the UNIX multitasking operating system. An understanding of how Shell programs work should help MS-DOS users when they become more sophisticated and require a multitasking operating system.

2. PC/IX

PC/IX was IBM's first microcomputer entry into the personal computer operating system market. PC/IX, however, consumed a large portion of the disk space on a PC/XT and lacked sufficient application software to make the operating system salable. PC/IX, a version 3 port of UNIX, was also too slow for personal computer users. The introduction of the PC/AT with a faster processor and more disk storage, however, led to the future of UNIX as a microbased operating system. The PC/AT ran both PC/IX and XENIX.

3. XENIX

XENIX began as Version 7 (AT&T's Version 1.7). Because of agreements between Microsoft and AT&T, there is little doubt that Microsoft will bring it up to System V for AT&T and IBM hardware environments. Some of the command names may be slightly different, but they should cause little confusion. As all UNIX system vendors strive to meet the standard and develop new software, XENIX and System V will set the de facto micro-operating system standards for all hardware.

XENIX comes with several different Shells: *sh, csh,* and *vsh. Sh* is the standard Bourne Shell. *Csh* is the Berkeley C Shell, which is similar to the C language in its constructs. The C Shell is useful for UNIX environments programming in C language. *Vsh* is the visual Shell—a simple interface for occasional users. XENIX offers a wide selection of Shells for different applications.

XENIX also offers commands to interface with DOS—Microsoft's Disk Operating System. These commands—*doscat, doscp, dosdir, dosls, dosrm, dosmkdir,* and *dosrmdir*—allow XENIX to operate with DOS files.

4.   AT&T'S UNIX SYSTEM V

AT&T has been running UNIX on DEC and AT&T hardware for 15 years. AT&T has also introduced a line of personal computers that run MS-DOS and UNIX. There is little doubt that these machines will be AT&T's flagship line for distributed UNIX processing. They will also interface well with AT&T's larger computers. The Bourne Shell is used in all these processors.

Any user logging on to a 3B2 or 3B5 will have a hard time discerning the difference between micro UNIX and minicomputer UNIX. The commands, Shell, and processing are the same. Shells written in one environment can be ported to the other without change. Productivity and quality benefit from using the same shells in each environment. Maintenance costs are low, because shells can be maintained centrally and installed in whatever machine needs them. Even Amdahl and Cray UNIX will be able to run unchanged Shell commands at some point in the future. This means that a micro UNIX-user will be able to learn in a small environment and then, as the need arises, move into larger systems without retraining or other problems.

5.   SUMMARY

Because of its portability and multitasking abilities, UNIX has quickly risen as a major competitor for the microcomputer operating system market. Both IBM and AT&T have a significant investment in UNIX for personal computers. Standards battles should rage for a while, but the Shell will always be at the center of UNIX's popularity. This book should help all micro users understand the philosophy and use of the Shell.

EXERCISES

1.   Name the currently available UNIX-like microcomputer operating systems.

2. Name the three Shells available on the various micros.

3. Describe the similarities between MS-DOS and UNIX.

4. Describe the benefits of UNIX as a microcomputer operating system.

CHAPTER

7

User Friendly Interfaces

Invariably, novice UNIX users come with some excess baggage. They know some other system, whether it's IBM's TSO, Honeywell, micros, or whatever. The UNIX Shell will seem foreign to them. Its concepts will seem awkward and unwieldy. Creating user friendly interfaces and lookalikes are the easiest ways to shorten a new user's learning curve.

By the time this book is in print, a variety of user friendly menus and windowing software packages should be available for UNIX. These should be acquired and implemented to encourage users to learn UNIX. Later, as they gain familiarity, they will begin to use more of the native commands. But what else can be done to encourage rapid learning?

1. CREATING LOOKALIKES

The link (*ln*) command and the Shell provide opportunities to make life easier on the new UNIX user. UNIX gurus may feel that these

crutches are unnecessary, but consider that the learning curve for a
new UNIX user may extend for a year or more. It makes sense to
shorten this curve in any way possible.

The link command can be used to link a UNIX command to a command name that the user already knows. For example, an IBM TSO
user knows the list command as *listc,* the line editor as *edit,* and the
full screen editor as *spf.* To make it easy on them initially, the system
administrator can link the UNIX list (*ls*), line editor (*ed*), and full
screen editor (*vi*) to the TSO command names:

```
cd /bin
ln ls listc
ln ed edit
ln vi spf
```

Similarly, a DOS user could learn more easily with the following
changes:

```
ln ls dir
ln ed edlin
ln vi spfpc (or whatever)
```

For a slightly more friendly interface, shells can be created to inform the user of what the system is doing for them when they execute a
command:

```
# edlin
echo "edlin is a DOS command."
echo "initiating the UNIX editor--ed"
ed $*
```

Creating these lookalikes can also be handled by two special facilities of the C Shell and Bourne Shell: *alias* and functions. In the C Shell,
the *alias* command lets the user create an alias for any command. The
same can be done with the Bourne Shell (UNIX System V Release 2
and later versions) using Shell functions.

The C Shell *alias* command takes the form:

```
alias command-name command(s)
```

The previous examples using the link command could have been handled equally well using *alias:*

```
alias dir "ls"
alias edlin "echo Initiating UNIX editor (ed);ed"
```

Alias could also be used to generate a horizontal listing of a directory's contents:

```
alias hls "ls : pr -t -5"
hls
bin      doc      src
```

The *alias* can also rename more complex commands that are contained in external C Shell files. The C Shell command to read and execute an external command is *source*. Use it with *alias* to include external files:

```
alias command-name "source external-command"
```

These *alias* commands should be included in the user's .cshrc file. When the user logs in, the C Shell will automatically evaluate the *alias* commands and make them available to the user.

Similarly, the Bourne Shell allows the user to establish an alias, but the means are different. The user must create a function. Shell functions should be included in the user's .profile for automatic invocation by the Shell. The previous examples are implemented as follows:

```
dir() {
ls $*
}
```

```
edlin() {
ed $1
}

hls() {
ls $* ! pr -t -5
}
```

Functions are not restricted to a single line as are *alias* commands. They can include loops, *if-then-else* decisions, or whatever. But the *alias* command can include Shell source from anywhere in the system. So, it can effectively implement anything that the Bourne Shell can.

Functions are executed directly by the Shell, so rather than *exit*, they must *return* or the Shell will exit, logging the user off.

```
oops() {                          okay() {
    shell commands . . .              shell commands . . .
    exit 0                            return
}                                 }
```

As shown in these examples, the C Shell's *alias* command and the Bourne Shell's functions give the user a flexible way to define user friendly names for any system commands.

The C Shell and the Bourne Shell also let users build specialized commands to make their jobs easier as well as more ergonomic. Shell commands should be written to automate most of the commands that users have learned on other systems. Additional Shell commands should be written to simplify man-machine interfaces. A simple example involves a command to clear the terminal screen depending on terminal type:

```
# clear terminal screen
case $TERM
    vt100'5420)                          # vt100 compatible
        echo "\033[;H\033[2J"
        ;;
```

```
    TV912)                                  # TELEVIDEO 912
        echo "\032\n"
        ;;
    *)
        echo "Do not know how to clear $TERM"
        ;;
esac
```

Clearing the screen and painting lines on the screen from the top down is much easier on the eyes than watching each new line scroll up from the bottom of the screen. Stationary lines at the top of the screen are easier to read than lines jumping up from the bottom every split second. The *clear* command can be executed from any other Shell command that needs it:

```
# anyother shell
    shell commands . . .
    clear                          # clear the screen
    display information
```

To extend the concept of friendly commands, the more exotic commands available on systems other than UNIX can be implemented in Shell. Commands that handle SCCS, RJE, and other UNIX programming facilities fall into this category.

2.   SCCS

The Source Code Control System (SCCS) maintains all versions of a document, source code, or whatever. The available SCCS commands are shown in Figure 7.1.

Working with UNIX and SCCS (Source Code Control System), you are fortunate to be working with one of the best configuration management tools available on any system. SCCS stores C-language code, documents, shells, or anything consisting of text and provides version control of virtually all UNIX text files. SCCS relieves the user of the effort of maintaining versions of a file manually. It also encourages

admin —add a file to SCCS

cdc   —change the *delta* commentary of an SCCS file

comb   —combine two versions of an SCCS file

delta   —create a new version of an SCCS file

get   —get a file out of SCCS

prs   —print description of an SCCS file

rmdel   —remove a delta from an SCCS file

sccsdiff—compare versions of an SCCS file

val   —validate an SCCS file

what   —look for *what* strings

Figure 7.1   SCCS commands.

quality control and security by use of its many and varied features. When developing new shells or C-language programs, store early working versions in SCCS so that you can recover them later if required. When changing a program, get the source code out of SCCS, change it, store it back, and then build the program from the SCCS source.

SCCS can hold all versions of a program, from its infancy through adulthood, until it is scrapped. It does so by keeping all versions of the source file in a single SCCS file. An SCCS file consists of SCCS control information, the initial version of the text, and all changes to the file as shown in Figure 7.2. Most other library systems will only hold the most current version of the source; the older versions are backed up on tape somewhere.

SCCS controls the growth of a program or document in a way that matches the maintenance of computer software: the initial development calls for incremental testing versions, an initial release, enhancements in future releases, and software fixes to existing releases. The trunk of the SCCS tree handles all releases of the system, while branches allow for fixes to already released software (Figure 7.3). The original version and every change to an SCCS file have an associated SCCS identification string (SID):

release.level or release.level.branch.sequence

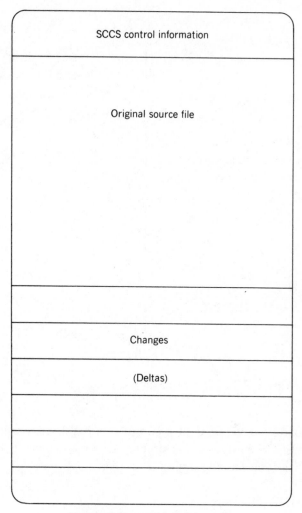

Figure 7.2 SCCS file layout.

Changes on the trunk of the tree have only a release and level number. The original version of the file typically has a release and level number of 1.1. Maintenance fixes to released software require the creation of a branch delta. Branches always contain all four parts of the SID. For example, a maintenance change made between levels 2.2 and 2.3 would have 2.2.1.1 as an SID.

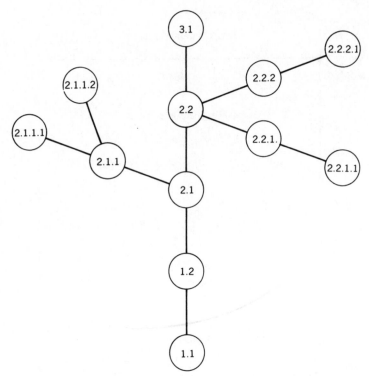

Figure 7.3   SCCS branching from the main text file.

Recovering old versions of files under other library systems is no fun. With SCCS, however, it is simple. All a user needs to do is *get* the file using the release flag (-r):

get -r3.2 s.filename

Even programmers on single-user systems will find SCCS of im-measurable value for controlling changes to software and documenta-tion.

SCCS has another facility that can improve the auditability of Shell, C, or any other kind of programming language. SCCS keywords can be embedded in the source code and expanded at the time that production versions of the programs are pulled from SCCS.

SCCS keywords are of the form %A%. The capital letter in the middle has a special meaning and the whole string is expanded when the user issues a *get* command. The various meanings of these keywords are shown in Figure 7.4. The keyword %Z% is of special interest. It is a shorthand notation for the string "@(#)", recognizable by *what*. The keyword %A% expands to %Z%, the module type (%Y%), the module name (%M%), and the SID (%R%.%L%.%B%.%S%). It should be included in every Shell program as a comment (see Appendix A):

SCCS ID %A%

Keyword	Description
%A%	Shorthand for %Z%%Y% %M% %I%%Z%
%C%	Current line number in the SCCS file
%D%	Current date—YY/MM/DD
%E%	Date of most recent delta—YY/MM/DD
%F%	SCCS file name s.filename
%G%	Date of most recent delta—MM/DD/YY
%H%	Current date—MM/DD/YY
%I%	SCCS ID (SID)—%R%.%L%.%B%.%S%
%R%	Release number
%L%	Level number
%B%	Branch number
%S%	Sequence number
%M%	Module name (file name)
%P%	Fully qualified SCCS file name (/unix/sccs...
%Q%	Value of -fqtext entered by admin
%T%	Current time—HH:MM:SS
%U%	Time of most recent delta—HH:MM:SS
%W%	Shorthand for %Z%%M% %I%
%Y%	Module type from -fttype entered by admin
%Z%	What string "@(#)"

Figure 7.4   SCCS keywords.

When retrieved from SCCS to create a production version of a program or document, the keywords are expanded to their values. *What* can then extract the keyword information from the file, providing a simple help facility:

```
get s.mycmd              # get the file, expand keywords˙
what mycmd               # print the keyword information
Shell mycmd 2.3.1.2
```

With embedded SCCS keywords, a system administrator can find the type, name, and version of every command in a directory.

SCCS files can be kept in any directory, but they should not be kept in the directory (i.e., /local/bin) with the executable commands; it is too inefficient. For convenience, it is best to store them in one location so that shells for accessing them can be built easily. Normally, they are stored under a directory called "sccs," which can exist under the user's home directory or the group's file system (Figure 7.5). Some users prefer to store documentation with the program and others favor a separate directory. Once the organization of SCCS directories is decided, Shell interfaces are easily created to add or change SCCS files.

The command to add files to SCCS is *admin*. It has a variety of

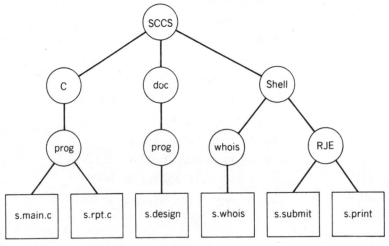

Figure 7.5   SCCS directory structure.

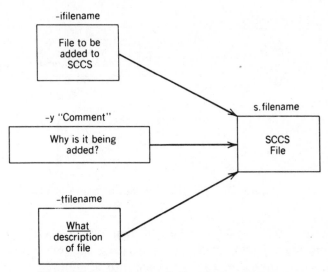

Figure 7.6 Diagram of the *admin* command.

options that are often unclear to new users. The command to add a file to SCCS, as shown in Figure 7.6, is as simple as:

admin -n -ifilename -y"First Release" -tdescription s.filename

Admin also lets the user specify who can have access to the SCCS file. By using the "-a" flag and a username or group number, the originator can specify those individuals who have the right to edit and update the SCCS file:

admin -n -ifilename -alja s.filename   # only I can update
admin -n -ifilename -a43 s.filename   # only group 43 can update

Once a file has been added to SCCS, the specified users will need to retrieve the file for enhancements and maintenance. The command to get files from SCCS is called *get*. Before retrieving the file, however, the user must decide whether he or she wants the file for editing purposes or just to browse the source. To make changes to an SCCS file, it must be retrieved with the edit flag (-e):

get -e s.filename

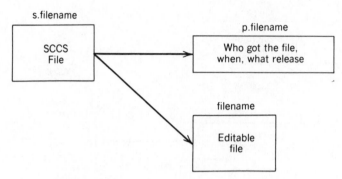

s.filename

p.filename

Figure 7.7 Diagram of the *get* command.

This creates two files: p.filename and filename. (See Figure 7.7.) The p.file contains an audit trail of who checked the text out and when. Until this user puts the SCCS file back into the library, no other user can get the file out for editing.

To browse the file or compile a production version, omit the edit flag:

get s.filename

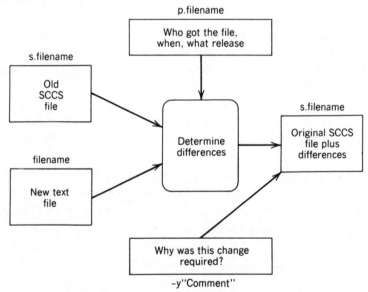

Figure 7.8 Diagram of the *delta* command.

To put the edited file back into SCCS, the user needs the *delta* command. The command to store a file back in SCCS (see Figure 7.8) is entered as follows:

delta -y"Reason for the change" s.filename

These simple commands will suffice for the simple user, but when the task requires controlling hundreds of Shell programs and documentation, the files should be kept in special SCCS directories and created or changed by use of Shell commands. A simple Shell interface to add files to these directories would accept the type of file, program name, and source name and add the file as follows:

```
#sccsadd type program file
if [ $# -eq 3 ]                # got all of the arguments?
then
   type=$1
   program=$2
   file=$3
else                           # prompt for the arguments
   echo "Enter Type: "
   read type
   echo "Enter Program Name: "
   read program
   echo "Enter File Name: "
   read file
fi
# name of type directory
typedir=$HOME/sccs/$type
# name of program directory
progdir=$HOME/sccs/$type/$program
if [ ! -d $typedir ]           # non-existent type directory
then
   mkdir $typedir              # create it
fi
```

```
if [ ! -d $progdir ]              # non-existent program directory?
then
   mkdir $progdir                 # create it
fi
echo "Enter one line description"
read description
#                                 ADD the file to SCCS
admin -n -i$file -y"${description}" ${progdir}/s.$file
```

The user could add a program to SCCS easily with the following command:

```
sccsadd c prg1 main.c
```

Similarly, to edit an SCCS file would require the following command:

```
#sccsedit type program file
if [ $# -eq 3 ]                   # got all of the arguments?
then
   type=$1
   program=$2
   file=$3
else                              # prompt for them
   echo "Enter Type: "
   read type
   echo "Enter Program Name: "
   read program
   echo "Enter File Name: "
   read file
fi
sccsfile=$HOME/sccs/$type/$program/s.$file
```

```
if [ -r $sccsfile ]                    # Does the SCCS file exist?
then
   get -e -s $sccsfile                 # go get it
else
   echo "File $sccsfile does not exist"
fi
```

To put the changed file back into SCCS requires a similar command:

```
#sccssave type program file
if [ $# -eq 3 ]
then
   type = $1
   program = $2
   file = $3
else
   echo "Enter Type: "
   read type
   echo "Enter Program Name: "
   read program
   echo "Enter File Name: "
   read file
fi
sccsfile = $HOME/sccs/$type/$program/s.$file
if [ -r $sccsfile ]
then
   echo "Enter one line description of change"
   read comments
   delta -y"$comments" $sccsfile
else
   echo "File $sccsfile does not exist"
fi
```

Creating user friendly interfaces to SCCS is one simple way to help programmers use SCCS easily, effectively, and consistently. Other user friendly interfaces can be built around the other SCCS commands to make programmers, analysts, technical writers, or whoever more productive. Another UNIX subsystem that requires some skillful handling is the Remote Job Entry facility (RJE), for programmers sending jobs to an external host machine.

3. RJE

UNIX is an excellent environment for developing software for UNIX as well as other host processors. Ninety percent of the programming task can be accomplished in UNIX, and then the product can be shipped to a number of different host processors for compilation and testing. The host may be a microprocessor, a minicomputer, or a mainframe (Figure 7.9). The UNIX Remote Job Entry (RJE) facility is the link to IBM mainframes. The available RJE commands are shown in Figure 7.10.

Most IBM users are used to the *submit* command in a TSO programming environment. What is it called in UNIX? *Send.* So, the most obvious way to handle IBM users shifting into a UNIX environment is to build a simple interface, called *submit,* around the *send* command.

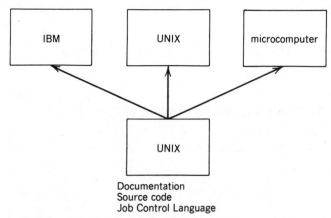

Figure 7.9 The UNIX programming environment.

dd   —convert ASCII files to EBCDIC or the reverse
gath   —gather JCL and data files together but do not send
rjestat—check the status of the RJE link
        or send JES or HASP requests to the IBM host
send   —send a job over the RJE

Figure 7.10   RJE commands.

The interface could be handled simply with the *alias, ln,* or function capabilities of the various Shells. Rather than submit JCL (Job Control Language) files directly via send, it is better to assemble jobs from common JCL files for job cards and the various processes required by a programmer (Figure 7.11). IBM JCL language consists of four basic types of statements:

1. JOB—JOB cards specify the user, password, and so on.

2. EXEC—Execute a specified program.

3. DD—Data definition (tape, disk, card, printer).

4. data—card input for various uses.

The format for each may vary from installation to installation, with differences in operating systems, hardware, and other elements.

A programmer may require hundreds of JCL files to compile, test, and create data for the programs he or she maintains. Operating system changes, compiler changes, database management system changes, or procedure changes can make any or all these files obsolete. Often the programmer will have to change each JCL file individually to continue working. Multiply this by possibly hundreds of programmers and the loss of productive work can be quite high.

Instead of forcing each programmer to keep up with these changes, the UNIX system administrators can keep the common JCL files up to date. The user friendly version of the *submit* command then isolates the programmers from the complexities of JCL and from changes in the operating environment.

To do this, *submit* must be capable of handling the three functions of program development: compiling, linking, and testing. Because of the

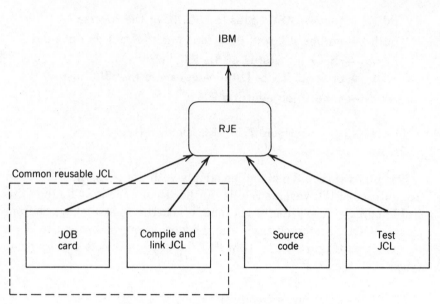

Figure 7.11 The UNIX RJE facility.

many differences among host system JCL requirements, compilers, test facilities, and so on, it would be impossible to show all the Shells required to handle all functions of the RJE. The following, however, is a short list of the commands required to make programming more productive.

   submit—send a compile, link, or test to the host

   fetch—get a file from the host

   put—put a file back on the host

   print—print a UNIX file on the host

   format—print a document on a laser printer attached to the host

The *submit* command should handle most of the user's JCL needs: creating a system standard JOB card, including EXEC and DD cards for the compiler and linkage editor job steps, and allowing the user to enter the name of a file containing the EXEC and DD cards to test the program. Figure 7.11 shows how the *submit* command should pick up each of the various JCL files. Once the files are gathered, they can be

sent to the host system using *send*. Since the JOB card routine is
needed by all the previously mentioned RJE commands, it should be
developed separately and executed by every other command:

```
# submit [cobol,pl1] [-link(program)] [-test(testjcl)] program
. jobcd                          # create job card
if [ $1 = "cobol" ]
then
   . cobolcompile ${$#}          # append COBOL compile JCL
   shift
elif [ $1 = "pl1" ]
then
   . pl1compile ${$#}            # append PL/1 compile JCL
   shift
fi
type=`echo $1 ¦ cut -c2-5`
if [ $type = "link" ]
then
   . link $1                     # append link JCL
   shift
   type=`echo $1 ¦ cut -c2-5`
fi
if [ $type = "test" ]
then
   . test $1                     # append test JCL
   shift
fi
send jobfile                     # send the JCL to the host
```

In this way, the other required commands—fetch, put, print, and
format—can use the *jobcd* Shell too. When the system requirements
change, only the jobcd routine need change.

In addition to user friendly Shell interfaces to the RJE, the *send*
command allows the user some additional flexibility. The *send* com-

mand can interactively prompt the user for keywords like the job name, DD card names, passwords, and so on. The keyword facility of *send* makes this possible. The following example will prompt the user for the job name, account code, and password when *send* reads the file:

```
~?:JOBNAME
~?:CODE
~?:PASSWD
//JOBNAME JOB ACCT=(CODE),PASSWORD=PASSWD,TIME=(10,0)
```

The command "send jobcd" reveals the following actions:

```
    ?JOBNAME newtest
    ?ACCTCODE 123456
    ?PASSWD nopasswd
```

Send would generate the following JOB card:

```
//newtest JOB ACCT=(123456),PASSWORD=nopasswd,TIME=(10,0)
```

Send can also include other files and the output from Shell commands as part of the file to be sent:

```
    ~include_filename
    ~!nroff -cm document_file : col
```

The first example would open the file, include_filename, as input and insert the contents of that file into the JCL wherever the line existed in the JCL file. The second example would use *nroff* to format the document_file. The result would pass through *col* to remove reverse line feeds (RJE printers don't know about reverse line feeds). The output of the entire command line would be inserted into the JCL file.

These various keyword and input inclusion facilities give the programmers a unique tool for system development and maintenance. These facilities are also useful with *gath*—a command to gather files together, just like *send*, without submitting the jobs to the host processor. An example of using *gath* for other than RJE work can be found in Chapter 9.

The other thing that programmers need is a facility to monitor the progress of their jobs on the IBM mainframe. The *rjestat* command not only checks the status of the RJE link, but can also make RJE requests of the IBM host. The TSO facility to check on jobs is *st*—a batch job status. The UNIX system administrator should build a matching UNIX command using *rjestat*.

The RJE is a powerful facility for linking UNIX with IBM mainframes. Similar, but not standard, UNIX facilities are available to interface with a wide variety of hardware. User friendly commands that match the host commands will help improve productivity in a UNIX environment.

4. SUMMARY

The Shell is a powerful environment for building user friendly interfaces to the facilities of UNIX. Because each new UNIX user comes with excess baggage from previous systems he or she has used, it makes sense to use the Shell to shorten the learning process.

There are many ways of creating user friendly interfaces, from simple link and alias commands to more complex Shell programs to handle SCCS, RJE, and all the other subsystems of UNIX. With careful planning, the UNIX system administrator can reduce training costs and general complaining as new users begin learning the system. Users are the heart of any system and keeping them happy is of paramount importance.

EXERCISES

1. Describe the Bourne and C Shell facilities to rename existing commands to user friendly names.

2. Use these various commands and facilities to create UNIX lookalike commands for commands from any other system you are familiar with.

3. Describe the benefits of SCCS.

4. Create the *clear* command for your terminal.

5. Use *admin, get,* and *delta* to create an SCCS file for the *clear* command and to add another terminal type to its capabilities. Use *get* to retrieve a production version of the command.

6. Use the *what* command to extract the SCCS keyword information from the *clear* command just created.

7. Create a branch delta from the first version of the *clear* command stored in SCCS.

8. Describe the function of the RJE facility.

9. Use IEBGENER to print a UNIX file over the RJE.

8

Advanced
Shell Programming

The major concern of advanced Shell programming is not special tools, fancy techniques, nor exotic man-machine dialogues, but a concern for quality. Shell, like any other programming language, can be used elegantly or shoddily. Quality is the highest concern of a Shell guru. But what is quality?

Quality results from several program design factors: reliability, maintainability, reusability, efficiency, portability, and usability. Each has a place in advanced shells. Reliability is a feature of shells that rarely fail and always perform the correct actions. Maintainability ensures that a shell can be enhanced or repaired easily when the need arises. Reusability demands that Shell programs be as flexible and reusable as any other UNIX command. Efficiency relates to the machine resources used—the fewer the better, because new machines are expensive and the longer their purchase can be delayed, the better.

Portability is a key factor in the popularity of UNIX; shells should remain as portable as possible. Usability is a key feature of Shell: native UNIX is not that friendly, but Shell is the means to overcome that problem.

Advanced Shell programming is to ballet what hacking is to hockey. Quality, quality, quality. It is the essence of advanced Shell programming. The Shell, in its creator's wisdom, provides many facilities that encourage quality programming. The following sections discuss their use.

1.   RELIABILITY

The costs of reliability problems can be easily seen: scrap, defect investigation, rework, retest, downtime, and productivity losses. Scrap costs involve the machine and user time lost when a command fails or works incorrectly. Defect investigation is the time it takes to identify the cause of a defect in a Shell program. Rework includes the labor to fix and rerun the command. Retest includes the resources necessary to test a repaired command. Downtime is the cost of the user's inability to do his or her work. Productivity losses include all the costs of delaying work.

1.1.   Default Actions

One of the simplest default actions occurs when a user executes a command that requires certain input parameters. If the user executes the command without any parameters, a simple Shell command will exit with an error message. An advanced Shell program, however, will prompt for the missing arguments and only exit if the user interrupts the processing. A simple check for arguments is as follows:

```
case $# in       # Check the number of arguments
   0)   # not enough prompt for the input arguments
        echo "Enter file name"
        read filename

        ;;
```

```
    1)   # just enough
         filename = $1

         ;;
    *)   # many files
         filename = "$*"

         ;;
esac
for file in $filename
do
    whatever
done
```

Thus, if the user fails to give a file name on the command line, the shell will prompt for the missing information. On the other hand, if the user gives many file names, the shell will process each file. In either case, the shell prevents the scrapping of this execution of the command and the work of reentering the command with the proper arguments.

Variable substitution offers another means of taking default actions. Regardless of a Shell variable's value, a default value can be substituted, or the variable can be left unchanged. Invoking these defaults instead of using undefined variable names will help make any shell more reliable. Consider the output of the following commands:

	Output	${name} becomes
name = /usr/bin		
echo ${name}	/usr/bin	/usr/bin
echo ${name:-"/dev/null"}	/usr/bin	/usr/bin
echo ${name: = "/dev/null"}	/usr/bin	/usr/bin
echo ${name:?"Error"}	/usr/bin	/usr/bin
echo ${name: + "/dev/null"}	/dev/null	/usr/bin
name = "" # set name to NULL		
echo ${name}		
echo ${name:-"/dev/null"}	/dev/null	NULL

	Output	${name} becomes
echo ${name: = "/dev/null"}	/dev/null	/dev/null
echo ${name:?"Error"}	Error	NULL (exit program)
echo ${name: + "/dev/null"}		NULL

Omitting the colon (:) in any of these examples causes the Shell to
check only the variables' existence. The Shell will not check for a null
variable. In the previous example, the variable *name* is set, but has a
null value. The results change as follows:

```
name = ""        # set name to NULL
echo ${name}
echo ${name-"/dev/null"}      NULL      NULL
echo ${name = "/dev/null"}    NULL      NULL
echo ${name?"Error"}          NULL      NULL
echo ${name + "/dev/null"}    /dev/null NULL
```

Other examples of using default actions requires a look at the Shell
constructs IF-THEN-ELSE and CASE. To display the best Shell programming style, every *if* should have an *else* and every *case* should
have a default action:

```
if [ -r $filename ]
then
   process $filename
else
   while [ ! -r $filename ]
   do
      echo "File $filename does not exist"
      echo "Please enter the correct filename"
      read $filename
   done
   process $filename
fi
```

```
case $TERM in
  vt100)
    tabs
    ;;
  630)
    tabs
    TERM=450
    ;;
  # default
  *)
    echo "Setting up terminal as tty37"
    TERM=37
    ;;
esac
```

In either of these two examples, a default action prevents the unexpected from occurring. The absence of a default path is one of the hardest errors to find in programs. IFs without ELSEs and a CASE without a default are often suspect when a Shell program is unreliable.

Taking intelligent default actions is one of the cornerstones of UNIX philosophy. Advanced Shell programs echo that philosophy. Errors and faults are avoidable in most Shell programs—an extension of UNIX's philosophy toward reliability.

1.2. Fault Handling

Fault handling is another feature of the Shell. The two major commands that handle error detection and correction are *test* and *trap*. *Test* helps detect errors before they occur, while *trap* catches interrupts and takes intelligent default actions.

As shown in previous examples, *test* can check for the presence of files, directories, or devices. (See Figure 3.1.) It can compare the value of two variables or test the value of a single one. *Test* can prevent many errors from happening and thereby prevent scrap, rework, downtime, and productivity losses.

Some Shell programs are made to run in either foreground or background. A file run in the background should not interrupt the user with spurious errors. It should mail them for later reference. *Test* can help direct error messages to the terminal or the user's mail as follows:

```
# if the terminal is associated with standard input
if [ -t 0 ]
then
    echo "Execution message"
else
    echo "Execution message" : mail $LOGNAME
fi
```

Test can also check for the presence of a variable:

```
# if $1 is non-null
if [ "$1" ]
then
    process $1
else
    echo "Enter file name"
    read filename
    process $filename
fi
```

The importance of *test* is to detect problems before they occur and then take an intelligent default action.

Trap works with system interrupts like the break or delete keys. The most common interrupts are hangup (1), interrupt (2), quit (3), alarm clock (14), and software termination (15). All of the available interrupts are shown in Figure 8.1. For more information on each, look in the *UNIX User's Manual*, Section 2, under *signal*. Another useful interrupt (0) occurs at the successful termination of a Shell command. With it, *trap* can take default actions upon completion of the command.

0—normal termination
1—hangup
2—interrupt
3—quit
4—illegal instruction
5—trace trap
6—IOT instruction
7—EMT instruction
8—floating point exception
9—kill
10—bus error
11—segmentation violation
12—bad argument to system call
13—write on pipe with no receiving process
14—alarm clock
15—software termination signal

Figure 8.1 Software termination signals.

Trap is often used to clean up after a shell when it ends. Temporary files are created in /tmp, /usr/tmp, or the user's directory. Whether the command ends or is interrupted, these files should be removed:

trap "rm -f /tmp/tmp$$ tmp$$; exit 0" 0 1 2 3 14 15

Trap can also identify the last file processed when a process is interrupted:

trap "echo $filename ¦ mail $LOGNAME" 1 2 3 14 15

Trap can also ignore interrupts while the Shell does tricky stuff that is not easily fixed after the command has been interrupted and reset itself after the operation is complete:

```
trap "" 1 2 3 14 15        # ignore common signals
cp /tmp/tmp$$ /etc/passwd   # copy updated password file
trap 1 2 3 14 15           # reset signal traps
```

Trap can handle increasingly complex jobs as required. These few simple examples are a beginning. Reliability is integral to UNIX and fault handling with *trap* is an important method of achieving that reliability.

2. MAINTAINABILITY

Maintainability depends on quality factors called consistency, modularity, self-documentation, and simplicity. Consistency recommends doing things in the same way from shell to shell. Instrumentation gives indications of the success or failure of the shell as it processes its input. Modularity is one of the keys to the success of UNIX; Shell programs should be modular. Self-documentation assumes that the Shell program will document itself. Simplicity says it all: a simple command is easily understood, modified, and maintained.

One facet of maintainability that is difficult to quantify is programming style. The examples in this book attempt to present a "good" and consistent programming style. To improve consistency, use the skeletal Shell program in Appendix A as starting point for all Shell programs. It contains most of the information needed for good self-documentation and on-line help facilities. Indenting Shell control structures to show the structure of the program is another form of consistent programming style (see Figure 8.2). Programming style is also concerned with simplicity. Because of the wealth of operators available with UNIX, any required program can be created in a number of different ways. Only a few of those ways will be simple and easy to maintain. Programming style is also reflected in the use of program development tools, like SCCS, to make Shell programs easier to maintain.

As UNIX users become more sophisticated, they will begin to see new opportunities for the use of existing commands. This means that Shell commands, no matter how well written, will need to evolve to meet those needs. Keeping shells in SCCS (see Chapter 7) will help

```
IF-THEN-ELSE
  if [ conditions ]
  then
      process1
  else
      process2
  fi

CASE and SWITCH
  case $ variable in name1
    match1)
        process match1
        ;;
    match2)
        process match2
        ;;
    *)
        default processing
        ;;
  esac

FOR and FOREACH
  for variable in name1 name2 ...
  do
      process $variable
  done

WHILE and UNTIL
  while [ conditions ]
  do
      process
  done
```

Figure 8.2 Control structure indentation for readability.

track the evolution of a command. The reasons for changing the commands will be stored with the SCCS file, so there is no documentation to lose. A list of changes and their reasons are as close as the *prs* command. Furthermore, as one UNIX machine grows to two or three or three dozen, the process of administering changes to the system can be simplified by extracting commands only from the SCCS libraries.

Before the commands are stored in SCCS, however, they have to be developed. Self-documentation is an important part of that development. Comments can be inserted easily into the code; they can be on a line by themselves or after an executable statement. The pound sign (#) begins all comments:

```
# If the user supplies an argument use it
if [ "$1" ]
then
    process $1
else # prompt for an argument
    echo "Enter file name"
    read filename
    process $filename
fi
```

These comments are essential to program maintainability when Shell commands become more complex. If the developer is struggling to understand how all of the commands fit together to accomplish the task, just think what the person who later maintains it must think.

Just about every Shell programmer runs across some ways of doing things that are more elegant than others. Whenever possible, store up these methods and use them in new shells or use them to replace complex code in existing shells. Simplicity should prevail over complexity. Otherwise, it eventually becomes impossible to maintain all the existing shells without an army of Shell gurus.

Modularity was invented to keep things simple. Cars are made of small modular components. The parts are easier to design and build than complex hand-built components. The parts are also easier to replace when they fail. The same is true for Shell programs. Modularity improves maintainability.

Modularity can be obtained in two ways: simplifying processing and creating sub-shells. Any Shell program longer than two pages becomes increasingly complex. In some cases, the program can be simplified. The shell may have one central process with various input and output filters. A simple, modular design would be:

```
choose input filters
choose processing parameters
choose output filters
execute input filters ! major process ! output filters
```

An example of this modular program can be seen in Chapter 9.

Creating sub-shells allows the main shell to control the actions of several others to obtain the required result. Rather than write one huge shell, each sub-shell can do their unique part and then pass control back to the parent shell. Sub-shells are also an important feature of reusability.

Modular shells can execute as follows:

```
edit inputfiles
update datafiles
select reportdata
print reports
```

Each sub-shell creates outputs that are used by future processes. The sub-shells can also be executed individually when required.

Sub-shells can also be executed directly in-line with the parent shell's code so that the sub-shell can access and modify any of the parent's variables:

```
# parent shell
variable = /usr/bin
. subshell

# subshell
cd $variable
```

```
ls -l
variable = /bin
```

From a pure programming standpoint, this is somewhat dangerous because the subshell can change the parent's variables. Otherwise, the parent would have to export the variable for the sub-shell to have access to it:

```
# parent shell
variable = /usr/bin
export variable
subshell
```

In this example, sub-shell would have access to the variable but would not be able to change it. Also, any changes made by the sub-shell to the current environment (such as changing directories) would not affect the parent shell.

Making small modular Shell programs helps improve maintainability. Small programs are easily understood. Modular programs also benefit reusability.

3. REUSABILITY

One of the reasons that UNIX is so popular is that each command is modular and reusable. Each command can be mated with other commands easily via the *pipe*. In the process of building commands to automate repetitive tasks for the users, functions are repeated from shell to shell. Creating a separate shell for these functions improves maintainability (there is only one copy to maintain). All of the shells that need the reusable function can then invoke it as a sub-shell.

When using Shell to prototype C-language programs, reusable shells often indicate the need for reusable C programs as well. Current technology has demonstrated that as much as 80% of a program's code is reusable, leaving only 20% to develop uniquely. This can increase program development by a factor of 2–5.

A simple way of achieving reusability is to create a library of generic Shell programs that can be copied and then enhanced to fit the need. These skeletons should include all the quality features described in this chapter. A good skeleton for Shell development is contained in Appendix A. As described in Chapter 5, there are four basic types of program design: edit, update, select, and report. A reusable Shell skeleton can be built for each.

4. EFFICIENCY

UNIX runs on a wide variety of hardware, but it still concerns itself with efficiency. Spending money for additional hardware is never easy, so it makes sense to take efficiency into consideration whenever building a shell. Some efficiencies are handled by the system administrator; others are available to the common user.

The system administrator (super user) can set the "sticky bit" on a program. Once the program has been loaded into memory, a copy is retained until the system is brought down. Keeping a copy of the program means that it can be swapped in when requested rather than read from disk, thereby speeding up processing. UNIX programs that are used extensively in Shell programs should have their sticky bit set.

Each user can further improve efficiency by simple actions. The most obvious one is to run commands during non-prime time on multi-user systems. Commands can be queued via the *at* command (if it is available on your system). The *at* command can off-load the processor during prime time and improve response time. The following example would execute a Shell accounting report called *acctrpt* at 6 P.M. on Sunday:

at 6pm Sunday acctrpt

Shell efficiencies are directly affected by the number of variables, commands, and files. The number and order of bins searched for commands are often prime candidates for efficiency improvement. These two criteria are established by the PATH variable:

PATH = :/bin:/usr/bin:/global/bin

The search order for this PATH is the current directory, /bin, /usr/bin, and /global/bin. If the user rarely uses the current directory and almost always /global/bin, then efficiency can be increased by switching the search order:

PATH = /global/bin:/bin:/usr/bin::

Other users will put all possible bins into their PATH:

PATH = :/bin:/usr/bin:/global/bin:$HOME/bin:/usr/bin/graf . . .

To find the requested command, the Shell must search through many directories and hundreds of files. A simple solution is to invoke the Shell itself as a sub-shell with the expanded PATH list:

```
# home
PATH = $HOME/bin:${PATH} PS1 = "HOME> " sh $@
```

This command changes the PATH variable to include $HOME/bin and changes the user's prompt to "HOME> " so that he or she is aware of the change. When finished using commands in $HOME/bin, the user types a control(d) to exit from the sub-shell.

The user can also improve efficiency by reducing the number of temporary files used in a shell. The use of pipes and a better selection of commands can reduce the number of temporary files:

```
cut -f1,5 /etc/passwd > /tmp/tmp$$
pr -o8 -h "Password listing" /tmp/tmp$$
rm /tmp/tmp$$

cut -f1,5 /etc/passwd | pr -o8 -h "Password Listing"
```

In this example, the number of commands was reduced by one and temporary files were eliminated totally. Pipes do create temporary files of their own, but *pr* can begin executing as soon as the *cut* has passed a line to the pipe. Herein lies the advantage of the pipe.

This example also showed how programming style can reduce the number of commands required. Similarly, the commands *fgrep* and *egrep* can be more efficient than *grep* for special data selection requirements. Many commands are available in UNIX. Often, one can be substituted for several others, thereby reducing complexity and improving efficiency.

The number of variable names can also influence efficiency. But the advantages of having good variable names and using them to represent only one variable instead of many outweigh the efficiency considerations.

Version V Release 2, has a facility that allows users the same capabilities as the "sticky bit." This version of the Bourne Shell allows the use of shell functions. Shell functions can be included in the user's .profile or anywhere for that matter. Once a command containing the function is executed, the Shell retains a memory copy of the function for later execution. When the user executes the command again, the function is invoked from memory instead of from disk. Response time is much faster. Shell functions are formed as follows:

```
functname()
{
    Shell commands
}
```

Shell functions provide the fastest way to obtain a response for frequently used commands. For more examples, see Creating Look-alikes in Chapter 7.

Efficiency is still a concern in UNIX systems. As UNIX users learn more about the system, their ability to use its resources expand exponentially, making it hard to obtain enough hardware to satisfy their cravings. The commands *time* and *timex* can examine resource usage of commands and be used to improve efficiency. Efficiency is one way of ensuring that there will be plenty of resources for all.

5. PORTABILITY

Portability is another major concern of the UNIX system. Shell programmers should also be concerned because there are two different

Shells: C Shell and Bourne Shell. And there are many different versions of UNIX. The Bourne Shell was rewritten for UNIX Version 2.0, which means that Version 7 (AT&T Version 1.7) is incompatible with 2.0 in many cases. The C Shell and Bourne Shell are also incompatible in many of their control constructs. These incompatibilities raise portability issues.

Every UNIX system seems to develop new tools that are not part of standard UNIX. These are then used in Shell programs, and those programs lose their portability. Binary copies of UNIX sold by third parties often have nonstandard utilities that are not portable to other systems.

To maximize the likelihood that shells can be ported from one machine to another, stick to the standard UNIX commands contained in /bin and /usr/bin. A Shell command using any other commands will need some work when moved from a micro- to a minicomputer or mainframe environment.

6. USABILITY

Probably the major problem with UNIX is its usability. Users complain of cryptic commands and so on. Shell is the bridge to improve usability. The best shells need default actions, help facilities, and possibly on-line instruction.

Usable Shell commands do not give cryptic error messages and exit when the argument list is deficient. They should prompt for the proper information as described in the reliability section of this chapter. Usable Shell commands should anticipate the user's needs and meet them wherever possible. The use of the *trap* command to handle interrupts is another means of making a shell more usable; a shell that cleans up after itself and restores order before exiting is more usable than one that does not.

On-line help facilities are another usability concern. The files contained in /usr/lib/help are not very beneficial, but they can be beefed up by the system administrator. Some people feel that the manual pages (man commandname) solve the problem, but they are too slow for maximum productivity. Extracting the meat of the manual pages and placing them in /usr/lib/help is the best solution to on-line help for the UNIX commands.

The Berkeley system has a command to help users find what they need. It is called *apropos*. It takes common words and looks up the various UNIX commands that might be related:

apropos list
ls - list a directories contents

User-developed Shell commands have other possibilities. Embedding help information in the Shell command is a good way to improve self-documentation and provide help facilities for locally developed commands.

Since shells should be stored in SCCS, the *what* command provides a facility for extracting help information from shells. The *what* command extracts lines from files containing the SCCS keyword string "%Z%" which expands to @(#). This keyword can be embedded in Shell commands:

 # %Z% syntax: command [parameters] [files]

which expands as follows when the file is retrieved from SCCS:

@(#) syntax: command [parameters] [files]

What can examine the Shell file and produce the following:

syntax: command [parameters] [files]

Grep can also be used. Some users will require just a simple example of the command's syntax; others will need more extensive assistance. Two levels of help information can be provided by combining *grep* with *what:*

#localhelp
grep "@#@" $1   # print syntax line
echo "More Information?"
read answer

```
if [ ${answer} = "y" ]
then
   what $1                        # print extended description
fi
```

Examples of the *grep* and *what* strings are shown in Appendix A. The local help command can be enhanced to look for the command in any of the bins specified by $PATH:

```
bins = `echo $PATH ¦ tr ":" " "`     # remove : delimiters
bins = "$bins `pwd`"                 # add current directory
for dir in $bins                     # check each bin
do
   if [ -r ${dir}/$1 ]               # if command exists
   then
      localhelp ${dir}/$1            # print help information
      break                         # leave FOR loop
   fi
done
```

This help command can be enhanced as required. On-line help for Shell commands, as shown in these commands, is a necessary part of productive use of UNIX. Usability is a major factor in the acceptance of UNIX and new commands. On-line tutorials, like the ones available with microcomputer packages, will be essential to reduce the training costs for new users. Local commands should take advantage of these packages to ensure that proper training is received by one and all. Training is a major part of usability. Developing a shell is often easy. Creating help and training materials often takes longer, but is perhaps more important than the resulting shell.

7. SUMMARY

Advanced Shell programming is concerned with the quality of the programs produced. It demands reliability, maintainability, reusability, efficiency, portability, and usability. A shell could be complex and intricate, a brilliant piece of work, but without self-documentation and maintainability, it cannot be what I call *advanced*.

The following chapters will demonstrate many features of the Shell that contribute to quality. Appendix A contains a skeleton of a shell that can be used to improve reliability, maintainability, and usability. The principles that involve advanced Shell programming are not ones of complexity, but ones of simplicity and elegance.

EXERCISES

1. What one thing is the major concern of an advanced Shell programmer?

2. What are the major factors that make up quality?

3. What is, in your words, programming style?

4. What Shell commands and features help provide reliability, maintainability, reusability, efficiency, portability, and usability?

5. Write a Shell program to test the various default values assigned to a variable that is:
   a. not set,
   b. set but has no value (NULL),
   c. set and has a value.

6. Write the *trap* command to ignore the interrupt and quit signals. Use it in a Shell command and test its performance with the break or delete key on your terminal.

7. Write a Shell command for the Bourne Shell systems to provide the equivalent of the Berkeley *apropos* command. Use a file of command names and their descriptions as input.

CHAPTER

9

===============

Handling Documents

Documentation is one of the major features of UNIX. The major documentation commands are shown in Figure 9.1. Using *nroff* and *troff,* the two major UNIX documentation commands, can be made much easier by use of Shell. Because of the number of commands and terminals that work with these two commands, it is often confusing to get all of the commands put together to generate the correct output. Shell helps eliminate those problems.

Otherwise, formatting documents with *nroff* would be as simple as:

nroff document_file

Usually, however, it takes many parameters and a few input and output filters to format a document correctly. The most frequently used parameters invoke a macro package.

checkeq —check a document's usage of equation macros
checkmm—check a document's usage of mm macros
col   —process nroff output for terminals with no reverse line
            motions
cw   —prepare constant width text for troff
deroff   —remove nroff macros
diffmk   —mark differences in two versions of a document
eqn   —equation preprocessor
gath   —gather files
greek   —prepare output for a special terminal type
lp   —spool output to printers
man   —format UNIX manual pages
mm   —format documents using Memorandum Macros
mmt   —typeset documents, view graphs, and slides
neqn   —equation preprocessor
nroff   —format documents for ASCII terminals
ptx   —generate permutated index
spell   —check spelling of documents
tbl   —table preprocessor
tc   —phototypesetter simulator for the Tektronix
troff   —format documents for a phototypesetter

Figure 9.1   Documentation commands.

1. MACRO PACKAGES

A number of macro packages have been designed to handle most documentation problems. These packages are contained in /usr/lib/tmac and /usr/lib/macros. The most common ones are the Memorandum Macros (mm) and manual page macros (man). The available macro packages are shown in Figure 9.2. They are further described in Section 5 of the *UNIX User's Manual*. Typically, a separate Shell command is necessary for each different macro package.

man —manual page macros
mm —memorandum macros
mosd—operations systems deliverable documentation macros
mptx —permutated index macros
mv —view graph and slide macros

Figure 9.2 Documentation macro libraries.

They are easily invoked:

nroff -mm document
nroff -man manpage

To speed up loading of the macros and to improve efficiency, use the compacted macros—a "compiled" version of the macros:

nroff -cm document
nroff -can manpage

Documentation problems that couldn't be solved easily with these macro packages required special preprocessors to prepare the input files for *nroff*. Commands were developed to handle tables and equations.

2.   INPUT FILTERS

The commands that preprocess *nroff* files are *eqn, tbl,* and *gath. Eqn* processes equations for mathematical output. *Tbl* creates the *nroff* macros needed to format tables. And *gath,* which normally works with the remote job entry (RJE) facility (see Chapter 7), can be used to set keywords, include files, or execute commands and use their output as input to *nroff* or *troff.* Each of these commands expands the capability of *nroff* for text formatting.

2.1.   *Eqn*

Eqn preprocesses mathematical equations for *troff*. Its twin, *neqn,* processes equations for *nroff*. They are useful for serious scientists, but hold little value for the average user.

They are invoked as input filters to *nroff* or *troff*:

> **eqn files : troff**
> **neqn files : nroff**

For the average UNIX documentation user, *tbl* and *gath* hold more interest.

2.2.   *Tbl*

Tbl takes files of the form shown in Figure 9.3 and turns them into usable input for nroff. The resulting output from the following command is also shown in Figure 9.3.

> **tbl document : nroff**

```
.TS
center tab(:) ;
l c c c
l n n n.
Sales:January:February:March
—
Southwest:100:110:120
Northwest:230:150:170
.TE
```

Sales	January	February	March
Southwest	110	110	120
Northwest	230	150	170

Figure 9.3   Documentation example using *tbl* macros.

On any system, *tbl* is a hog. It is more efficient to check the file for tables than it is to use *tbl* on all documents. Use *grep* to check the file:

```
# get the names of any files that have tables
if [ -z `grep -n "^.TS" $* ! line` ]
then
    nroff -cm $*            # no tables in the file
else
    tbl $* ! nroff -cm      # process tables and format file
fi
```

Invoking the *grep* command takes less time than running *tbl* on every file. It also keeps the user from forgetting to invoke the table preprocessor when required. Both of these advantages make the cost of searching each file for tables an inexpensive proposition.

2.3. *Gath*

Gath (see Chapter 7) gathers information together just like the *send* command, but it doesn't send the information over the RJE. Instead, it puts the output on stdout. *Gath* can preprocess text to prompt for keywords, include files, and execute commands.

Keywords are useful when the document doesn't change, but certain key phrases do:

```
~ = :FIRST
~ = :LAST
~ = :ADDRESS
~ = :CITYSTZIP
.nf
FIRST LAST
ADDRESS
CITYSTZIP
.sp
Dear FIRST,
```

```
.sp
.fi
. . . letter
```

gath letter ! nroff -cm

```
FIRST = Jay
LAST = Arthur
ADDRESS = 123 Anystreet
CITYSTZIP = Anytown, AZ 12345
```

Gath will prompt for each keyword, as previously shown, and then substitute them for all occurrences. The keywords can also be supplied on the command line:

```
FIRST = Jay LAST = Arthur ADDRESS = "123 Anystreet" \
CITYSTZIP = "Anytown, AZ 12345" gath letter ! nroff -cm
```

Gath can also include files in the text:

```
text
~filename
text
```

Gath will include *filename* at that point in the text. *Nroff* can also do this:

```
text
.so filename
text
```

The *nroff* version does have some advantages, however. For one thing, *gath* is not required, so efficiency is improved. For another, *nroff* creates a new and unique environment to process the new file before including it in with the existing text; *gath* does not. In rare instances this can cause problems.

But *gath* can also execute commands. In the following example, *gath* retrieves a file from SCCS and runs it through *tbl* before inserting the text in the file.

```
text
~!get -p s.tablefile ¦ tbl
text
```

Gath can even include the output from specific commands like ls:

```
text
~!cd;ls -l
text
```

These are trivial examples, but they illustrate the potential for pre-processing *nroff* and *troff* input to allow for more robust documentation. The presence of *gath* commands can also be detected with *grep:*

```
grep -n "~" $*
```

In cases where both *gath* and *tbl* are required as input filters, execute *gath* before *tbl* to ensure that all tables are included with the text before invoking *tbl*.

```
gath $* ¦ tbl ¦ nroff -cm
```

Once the input has been processed correctly, *nroff* or *troff* must be brought into play to format the resulting text in a way suitable for the output device.

3.   TERMINAL HANDLING

Because UNIX uses mainly asynchronous communications (except for rare implementations of synchronous support), innumerable types of terminals can be used with UNIX. Video display terminals vary from so-called "dumb" terminals to personal computers. Hard-copy output devices range from simple teletypes through dot-matrix and letter-quality printers as well as laser printers. Top quality laser printers, costing hundreds of thousands of dollars, are often connected to the host machine at the other end of the RJE link. These are all available to UNIX and connected as shown in Figure 9.4.

Because of the variety of output devices, *nroff* and *troff* use numer-

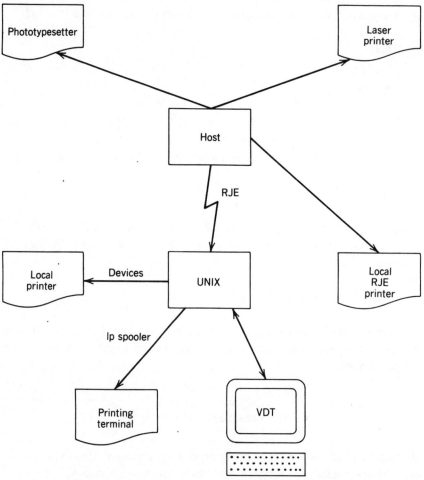

Figure 9.4   Printing options in a UNIX environment.

Nroff and Troff

-i	—read standard input after files
-n*n*	—number first page as *n*
-o	—print only the pages requested
-q	—use input/output mode of .rd request
-rA*n*	—set register A to *n*
-s*n*	—stop every *n* pages
-z	—print messages generated by .tm requests
-c*maclib*	—include the compacted macro library
-k*maclib*	—Compact the macros used and store them in the current directory as [dt].*maclib*
-m*maclib*	—include the named macro library

Nroff Only

-e	—invoke proportional spacing
-h	—use tabs to speed output
-T*name*	—output for terminal *name*
-u*n*	—set emboldening factor

Figure 9.5   *Nroff* and *troff* formatting options.

ous parameters to control their output (Figure 9.5). These two commands also extract a heavy toll from the system. In most active UNIX systems, *nroff* and the screen editors will consume most of the system's resources. All too often, a user entering an *nroff* command forgets to enter all the parameters needed and tries again and again to get everything "right" for the terminal. In the process, the user eats up too many system resources.

To circumvent this resource drain, it is usually wise to develop Shell commands that handle *nroff* or *troff* output to the various terminal types. The following sections describe using *nroff* with each terminal type.

3.1. Video Display Terminals

VDTs come in two screen widths: 80 and 132. To have *nroff* format the output correctly for comfortable viewing, the width and offset options must be set as follows:

nroff -r00 -rW79 document
nroff -r00 -rW131 document

Why are the line widths one less than the maximum length? Well, at the end of each line is a carriage return (CR) and line feed (LF). Most VDTs have what is called a wraparound feature—a long line is not truncated at the edge of the screen; a line feed is automatically generated and the remainder of the line prints on the next line on the screen. If the lines were 80 in length, a CR would generate a wrap-around LF and the LF following would leave a blank line on the screen. Line widths of 79 and 131 seem to work best. Since what people see on the screen should not differ from what ultimately prints on a printer, these width options should be used for all printer output as well.

Emboldening—making text appear darker—is possible with *nroff* and *troff*. *Nroff* emboldens text by overstriking each character as many as four times. The result of *nroffing* the following text is a series of characters and backspaces:

.B user
u<u<u<us<s<s<se<e<e<er<r<r<r

Since most VDTs switch into enhanced print via a control character sequence, all these backspaces and extra characters are unnecessary and require longer transmission times. Unless the administrators have developed an output filter to handle these special situations, suppress them by using the -u option to eliminate emboldening:

nroff -cm -u -rW79 -r00 document

This helps speed up the transmission of the formatted document. Most other adjustments to the output are handled with output filters.

3.2. Printing Terminals

Printers have only one important option. The type of printer should be specified with the -T parameter:

nroff -cm -T450 -rW79 -r08 document

This command specifies that the output is a Diablo printer (-T450) and that the output be offset 8 spaces to the right (-r08). The available terminal types on your system can be found by requesting:

help term2

Local line printers can receive output by I/O redirection of the nroff output into a device name or a spooler:

nroff -cm -T37 -rW79 -r08 document > /dev/lp
nroff -cm -T37 -rW79 -r08 document ¦ lpr
nroff -cm -T37 -rW79 -r08 document ¦ opr

Remote line printers must have the document sent over the RJE. Special processing is required to correctly format a document on a remote line or laser printer. Special processors include a variety of output filters.

4. OUTPUT FILTERS

The most common output filters for *nroff* are *col, pr, sed,* and *uniq*. All four are useful with VDTs. *Col* is also useful with some printers.

Col removes reverse line motions that are used to handle underlining, superscripts, and subscripts. VDTs and a few line printers cannot handle reverse line motions. So, *col* is used to convert reverse line motions into single-line combinations of backspaces and characters. *Col* removes super- and subscripts from *nroff's* output. The output of any *nroff* command for a video display terminal should be run through *col:*

nroff -cm -r08 -rW79 document ┆ col

For some reason, *col* generates underlining as the following: character, backspace, and then the underscore. The underscore overwrites the meaningful information. Some terminals do not allow backspaces, which causes other problems. Without writing specific C-language filters to handle each VDT's underlining and emboldening capabilities, it is best to eliminate backspaces and their ensuing character from the *nroff* output using *sed* as follows:

nroff -cm -u document ┆ col ┆ sed -e "s/\b.//g"

The output of *nroff* can be further optimized for screens by use of filters. The most obvious one is *uniq,* which suppresses duplicate lines. Duplicates are most often blank lines at the end of a page. At 1200 baud, a short last page can zip off the screen before the user can read it. To eliminate all but one occurrence of each blank line, use *uniq:*

nroff -cm document ┆ col ┆ sed -e "s/\b.//q" ┆ uniq

Another way to handle the problem is to present only 24 lines at a time and then allow the user to request more information with *pr:*

nroff -cm document ┆ col ┆ sed -e "s/\b.//" ┆ pr -l24 -t -p

Pr will sound the terminal bell and the user can hit return to view each new section of a formatted document. Other similar commands can do a more robust job of showing output than *pr,* but they are not included with System V UNIX. If the *more* or *pg* commands are available, they can be used to allow backward and forward scrolling through the output.

5. PUTTING IT ALL TOGETHER

Customizing document output for a particular terminal can be handled
with a variety of input and output filters. The command line for each
terminal type looks like this:

input filters ¦ nroff [macros] [parameters] ¦ output filters

To put all of these filters together requires changes to /etc/profile
and the creation of an output command. First, /etc/profile should ask
for the terminal type and assign it to the variable TERM:

```
echo "Enter Terminal Type: "
read TERM
case $TERM in
  vt100¦5420¦tv970)
    tabs
    ;;
  lp¦620¦630¦laser)
    ;;
  ti¦700¦745)
    tabs
    ;;
  *)
    echo "Setting up default terminal"
    ;;
esac
```

The user will be prompted for this information at login, and then the
output command can use $TERM to make intelligent default choices
for *nroff*. It should check for tables, equations, and commands for *gath*.
Then it should invoke output filters for the terminal type:

```
#   output file(s)
if [ $# -gt 1 ]                        # check parameter count
```

```
then
#      save the parameter entered by the user
   # flags
   while [ `echo $1 ¦ cut -c1` -eq "-" ]
   do
      # save flag
      parameters = "${parameters} $1"
      shift                          # delete flag
   done
#      check the files and save their names
   while [ "$1" ]                    # while more arguments
   do
      if [ -r $1 ]                   # readable file?
      then
         files = "${files} $1"       # save file name
      else
         echo "file $1 not found"
      fi
      shift                          # delete argument
   done
#      determine the input filters
   tblcnt = `grep -c "^.TS" $files ¦ cut -f2 -d: ¦ sort -nr ¦ line`
   gathcnt = `grep -c "^~" $files ¦ cut -f2 -d: ¦ sort -nr ¦ line`
   if [ $tblcnt -gt 0 ]
   then
         inputcnt = `expr ${inputcnt:=0} + 1`
   fi
   if [ $gathcnt -gt 0 ]
   then
         inputcnt = `expr ${inputcnt:=0} + 2`
   fi
   case $inputcnt in
      0)
```

```
          inputfilter = "cat $files ¦ "
          ;;
      1)
          inputfilter = "tbl $files ¦ "
          ;;
      2)
          inputfilter = "gath $files ¦ "
          ;;
      3)
          inputfilter = "gath $files ¦ tbl ¦ "
          ;;
      *)
          echo "Error in output: filters $inputfilter"
   esac
   case $TERM in
      vt100¦5420¦tv970)
          parameters = "$parameters -u -r00 -rW79 "
          outputfilter = " ¦ col ¦ sed -e "s/\b.//g" ¦ uniq"
          ;;
      lp¦620¦630)
          parameters = "-r08 -rW79 $parameters "
          outputfilter = ""
          ;;
      ti¦700¦745)
          parameters = "-r00 -rW79 $parameters "
          outputfilter = " ¦ col "
          ;;
   esac
   eval "${inputfilter} nroff ${macros: = "-cm"} ${parameters} \
      {outputfilter}"
else
   echo "No files specified"
fi
```

The actual make up of the *output* command will vary with the type of terminals in use. But the advantages of typing the simple command *output document* to print files should be obvious.

6.   SPOOLING DOCUMENTS

A line printer (*lp*) spooler was added to UNIX Version 4 and later versions. *Lp* allows the system administrator to define the types of printers on the system. Then each user can spool files to a printer without actually logging on. The printout can be picked up later at the user's convenience. *Lp* can even send the user mail when the file finishes printing.

To use *lp*, the printers have to be defined and labeled by the system administrator. Then documents can be spooled easily by creating a command to make a few decisions for the user. The spooler must decide whether to print an existing file or execute a command and print its output. A simple version looks like this:

```
# spool [files!commands]
if [ -r $1 ]      # readable file?
then
    lp $*         # print the file
else
# execute the command and print the resulting output
    trap "rm /tmp/tmp$$;exit 0" 0 1 2 3 14 15
    eval $* > /tmp/tmp$$        # execute the command
    lp /tmp/tmp$$              # print the output file
fi
```

Using *spool,* documents can be formatted with the *output* or *pr* commands, and printed by *lp:*

```
spool output document
spool pr -o8 textfile
```

In the first example, the *output* command will format the document file and *spool* will print the resulting file via *lp*. In the second example, *pr* will format the text file and *spool* will then print it via *lp*. Formatting requests that are more complex than those provided by the use of *output* and *pr* will require the use of other miscellaneous filters.

7. MISCELLANEOUS FILTERS

Figure 9.6 and 9.7 show the various filters available for handling documents with *nroff* and *troff*. Output filters for *nroff* that are occasionally

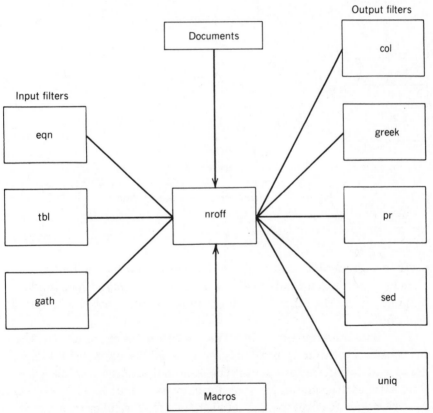

Figure 9.6   *Nroff* input and output filters.

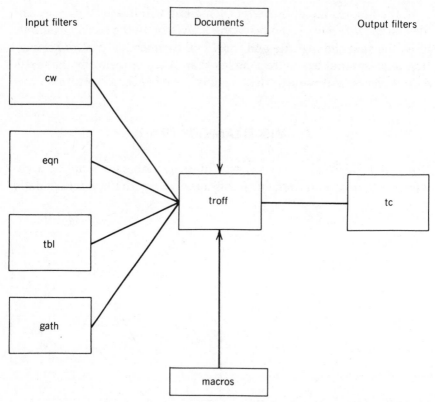

Figure 9.7   *Troff* input and output filters.

useful are *greek, 300,* and *450. Greek* turns output for the teletype 37 model printer into formats useful with a wide variety of nonstandard output devices. The other two filters can be invoked with the -T option of *nroff.*

Troff uses the same input filters as *nroff* with one exception: *cw. Cw,* the constant width preprocessor, uses some additional macros to handle special output requirements. The other output filter *troff* uses is *tc,* a phototypesetter simulator that formats its output for a Tektronix 4114 terminal. Each of these filters is handy for special circumstances, but most users will rarely need them.

8. MISCELLANEOUS COMMANDS

A number of commands that work with *nroff* text: *man, mm, mmt, deroff,* and *spell. Man* formats manual pages using a unique set of macros. It executes *nroff* with a variety of options to format the output.

Mm invokes *nroff* using the memorandum macros. It can do many of the things the previously developed Shell commands, like *output,* can do, but it lacks the robustness available with the Shell.

Mmt typesets slides and viewgraphs. If you have a 4114 terminal, it is worth playing with these macros.

Deroff removes all *nroff* and *troff* macros from a file, which is occasionally useful.

Spell is one of the most useful document processing tools. It finds most of the spelling errors in a document. *Spell* produces its list of errors one word per line. If there are extensive errors, the list will scroll off the screen quickly. A solution is to print the output of spell horizontally:

spell document ¦ pr -4 -w79 -e20 -i20

The Writer's Workbench facility also provides some excellent tools for examining and improving documents. Commands like *style* and *prose* can be beneficial to writers. Shell commands can be created to run all these commands against a document and print or store the results. These shells should be created as needed.

9. SUMMARY

Shell provides some excellent tools for handling documents and preparing them for output on the wide variety of devices available to UNIX. Connecting all these tools can improve efficiency and reliability: the user types one simple command and it determines how to format each document. Commands can be easily created for each set of *nroff* or *troff* macros.

Documentation is one of the strengths of UNIX. Full-screen word processors are available that will begin to displace *nroff* and *troff,* but there are still hundreds of thousands of *nroff* users who need simple interfaces to its facilities. Use the Shell to fill those needs.

EXERCISES

1. Describe the various input and output filters for:
    a. *nroff,*
    b. *troff.*

2. Describe the macro packages available for document preparation.

3. Write a while loop to use *gath* to enter names and addresses for inclusion in an *nroff* text file.

4. Use *spell* to check the correctness of any document in UNIX.

5. Write a Shell command to display the output of *nroff* on a terminal screen and pause between pages.

6. Use the commands in the Writer's Workbench to examine the style and prose contained in any UNIX document.

10

The Shell and
C-Language Programming

The Shell, especially the C Shell, is oriented to work with C-language programming. The Shell can assist in all phases of C-language development: prototyping, coding, compiling, and testing. The Shell provides the means to try out new ideas quickly and easily. C language is the vehicle to construct a program once its design has been established and tested with Shell.

1. PROTOTYPING

Chapter 5 described the four basic types of program designs: edit, update, select, and report. It also described the various tools available to a Shell programmer for implementing these designs. These tools can be used to develop a working version of any program design. The resulting Shell program is a prototype of the final working version that can be created in C language, or any other, for that matter.

One of the best design tools for describing new programs is the data flow diagram (Figure 10.1). Shell is one of the best tools for implementing a working model—a prototype—of a data flow. Because of facilities like pipes, tees, and input/output redirection, an idea can be prototyped in Shell, tested, changed as required, and then implemented in C. Many different designs can be tested, rejected, and accepted in a short time frame using Shell. The triumphant design can then be created in C language for efficiency reasons. In many cases, however, the Shell program will be sufficient. In the instances that require C programming, the program design evolved using the Shell will be more resilient and open to change.

Data flows have long been recognized as excellent methods of describing system, as well as program, designs (Stevens, 1982). Shell helps implement those designs. Prototyping, in a UNIX environment, works best with a small design team that is experienced with Shell programming. The result of such a design process is a simple, economy-grade working system.

The best Shell for prototyping C-language programs is the C Shell because of its C-like syntax. The Bourne Shell can be used, but its syntax does not translate directly into C-language. C Shell, on the other hand, provides an excellent pseudocode for C. The following example is a C-Shell prototype of a C-language main program:

C Shell	C Language
foreach file $argv[*]	main(argc,argv)
process $file	int argc; /* number of args */
end	char **argv; /* argument array */
	{
	int i = 0;
	for(i = 1;i<argc;i++) {
	process(argv[i]);
	} /* END FOR */
	} /* END MAIN /*

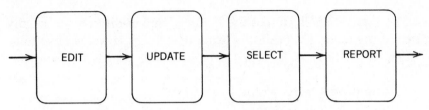

Figure 10.1 A simple data flow diagram.

The C Shell takes the complexity of data definition out of the program and allows the designer to concentrate on *what* the program should do rather than *how* it should be done. The C Shell serves as a clear design definition as well. C Shell prototypes can also be used to design and test enhancements to the program as they are required. The Bourne Shell could have been just as useful in this example:

```
for file in $*
do
    process $file
done
```

But the syntax is not exactly the same. Without argv[*] to represent the input parameters and some of the other features of the C Shell, the Bourne Shell lacks some of the clarity that the C Shell retains.

C Shell can also implement the use of tables and accessing the elements of those tables more effectively than the Bourne Shell:

```
set table = (John Jerry Terry)          static char **table = { "John",
                                            "Jerry", "Terry" };

foreach person table[*]                  for(i = 0;i<3;i++) {
    process $person                          process(table[i]);
end                                      }
mail $table[2] < letter                  sprintf(cmd,"mail %s < letter",
                                            table[2]);
                                         system(cmd);
```

The Bourne Shell, unlike the C Shell, cannot directly access any item in the table. To obtain the last name, Terry, it would have to be cut out of the list:

```
lastperson = `echo $table ¦ cut -f3 -d" "`
```

There are other advantages to the C Shell: The C-Shell CASE construct, switch, is identical to the C-language construct except that it will work with strings and the C-language switch only works on characters. The IF-THEN-ELSE construct is also identical to the C-language one. This parallel design allows quicker understanding and translation of designs into code.

The CASE construct translates into C-language differently depending on how it is used. If *switch* is used with characters or integers, the translation is identical:

```
switch $variable            switch(variable) {
    case a:                     case 'a':
        whatever                    whatever;
        breaksw                     break;
    case 10:                    case 10:
    case 11:                    case 11:
        whatever                    whatever;
        breaksw                     break;
    default:                    default:
        default action              default(action);
        breaksw                     break;
    endsw                   } /* END SWITCH */
```

When the switch works on strings, however, the C-language switch cannot be used. A series of IF-ELSEIF statements must be used along with the string comparison functions:

```
switch $variable            if(strcmp(var,"Jan") = = 0) {
    case "Jan":                 January();
```

```
        January              } else if(strcmp(var,"Feb")= =0) {
        breaksw                   February();
    case "Feb":               } else if ...
        February
        breaksw
    default:                  } else {
        default action            default(action);
        breaksw               } /* END CASE */
    endsw
```

Aside from the Shell constructs (IF-THEN-ELSE, CASE, FOR, and WHILE), just about anything else required of a C-language program can be implemented in Shell. Writing to a terminal and reading a response are easy with *echo* and *read:*

```
echo "Enter filename"      printf("Enter filename");
read file                  gets(file);
```

More complex processes, involving pipes and several commands, often translate into submodules in C language. For example, the best way to process the following command in C language is to open /etc/ passwd, match the name, and then print the required values:

```
grep lja /etc/passwd : cut -f1,5
```

In reading these examples, you should have seen the possibilities of using the Shell to prototype C-language programs. A rudimentary working system can be constructed quickly and tested easily. Different design choices can be evaluated and accepted or rejected. Design changes can be completed quickly before coding begins. As many as 80% of the errors in developed systems can be traced to problems in the design phase. Using Shell to weed out those problems can keep a software development project on track and produce a higher-quality product. Once coding begins, the Shell takes on other duties that aid in the development and maintenance of C language programs: coding, compiling, testing, debugging, configuration management, and release control.

2. CODING

As previously mentioned, the four major types of program designs are edit, update, select, and report. Each can be prototyped easily with Shell. Now begins the important task of translating the shells into C language. One of the best ways to speed up the process of writing C-language programs is to establish a directory containing skeletal programs of the four major program designs. These can be easily copied into the programmer's directory for expansion using Shell:

```
# proto skeleton newname.c
skeletondir=/global/C/skeletons
case $# in
  0!1)
     echo "Prototype List:\n"
     ls $skeletondir
     echo "Enter skeleton type"
     read skeleton
     echo "Enter newname.c"
     read cname
     ;;
  2)
     skeleton=$1
     cname=$2
     ;;
  *)
     echo "$0 syntax: $0 skeleton newname.c
esac
while [ ! -f ${skeletondir}/$skeleton ]
do     # prompt until they get a valid skeleton type
```

```
        echo "Skeleton $skeleton not found"
        echo "Enter skeleton type"
        read skeleton
        echo "Enter newname.c"
        read cname
done
cp $skeleton $cname      # copy skeleton to newname.c
echo "Skeleton module $cname has been created"
```

C or Bourne Shell skeletons of the four major program designs should be created and maintained for the prototyping staff. Reusing designs and code is much more productive than reinventing the wheel. Thus let the Shell handle as much of the typing and logic as possible. A simple C-language skeleton is shown in Appendix B.

Aside from the *proto* command which you can develop for your own use to speed up the coding process, UNIX provides a series of commands to aid the programming process. They are shown in Figure 10.2. These commands handle concerns like structuring the code for readability, printing the code, and documenting what the code does.

The C-language beautifier, *cb*, lets the programmer enter the code in any format and then transforms the code to one of several standard conventions. It straightens up the code and makes the logic more visible. The readability of the code is enhanced and so is the maintainability. *Cb* provides a consistent format for the code.

```
cb    —C-language beautifier
cflow—C-language flow analyzer
cref  —C-language cross reference (Version 3)
cxref—C-language cross reference
list  —print C-language listing
lint  —C-program checker
nl    —print a numbered listing
xref  —C-language cross reference (Version 3)
```

Figure 10.2 C-language coding commands.

List and *nl* provide two means of printing C-language listings. *List* works on object files that contain symbolic debugging symbols. *Nl* provides a numbered listing of C source code. Either can be combined with *pr* to produce a clean listing of a C program:

```
# clist cnames.c
for file in $*
do
    nl $file ¦ pr -o8 -h "Source listing for $file"
done
```

As programmers create programs, they often include datanames that are not used, statements that cannot be reached, or other problem code. *Lint,* the C-program checker, finds all kinds of stylistic problems and bug-prone code. The output produced by *lint* can be selected, cut, pasted, and reported in ways that help clean up the code before compilation. *Lint* also helps spot C-language portability problems when invoked with the "-p" option. *Lint* is an important tool in the development of portable, bug-free C-language programs.

Cflow and *cxref* help document how the program works (i.e., which module calls another, which datanames are referenced and where, etc.). *Cflow* works on any combination of C, yacc, lex, assembler, and object files. *Cxref* works only on C-language files.

By keeping all of the source code for a single program in a single directory, *cflow* can be executed simply as:

```
cflow *.[closy] ¦ pr -o8 -h "Cflow listing for program `pwd`"
```

Similarly, *cxref* can operate on all C-language files:

```
cxref *.c ¦ pr -o8 -h "Cross Reference for `pwd ¦ basename`"
```

The commands presented (e.g., *cb, cflow,* and *lint*) are not the only ones that can be used during the coding process, but they are the major ones. Inventive toolsmiths will find others that can aid the coding process. Once a program has been coded using the finest tools available, it must then be compiled and tested.

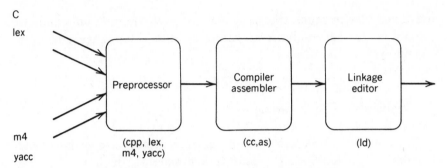

Figure 10.3 Steps in compiling a UNIX program.

3. COMPILING

C-language programs are created in three separate steps: preprocessing, compiling, and loading (Figure 10.3). The commands that perform these processes are shown in Figure 10.4. The Shell is the glue that links these commands together.

There are five major preprocessors for C-language: the C-language preprocessor *cpp* (invoked automatically by the C compiler), *lex* (generates lexical analysis programs), *yacc* (generates grammar analysis and parsing programs), *m4* (allows for macro substitution), and *regcmp* (compiles regular expressions for use with the function *regex*, which

as	—assembly language compiler
cc	—C-language compiler
dis	—object file disassembler
ld	—linkage editor
lex	—lexical analyzer preprocessor
make	—compile and assemble programs
m4	—macro preprocessor
regcmp	—compile regular expressions
strip	—strip symbol tables
yacc	—yet another compiler compiler preprocessor

Figure 10.4 Preprocessing and compiling commands.

THE SHELL AND C-LANGUAGE PROGRAMMING

examines text in much the same way as *grep*). Simple commands to preprocess lexical analyzer or *yacc* code into C-language and then compile it look like this:

```
lex file.l && cc lex.yy.c -ll
yacc file.y && cc y.tab.c
```

The *m4* macro processor was designed as a preprocessor for C and assembly code. It allows the definition of macros, which are then expanded by *m4* prior to compilation. Many of the abilities of *m4* are included in the C preprocessor. Only on rare occasions will a programmer need to use the macro preprocessor. Some of the assemblers (*as*), however, use *m4* as a preprocessor. It can be invoked whenever needed:

```
m4 file.m > file.c && cc file.c
```

The regular expression compiler, *regcmp,* performs most of the work done by the C function of the same name. It allows regular expressions to be compiled (an expensive process) before a C-language program is compiled or tested, thereby saving execution time. It creates an output file, *file.i,* which can be included directly into C-language code. Once compiled, regular expression analysis can be performed directly by *regex:*

```
regcmp regfile && cc file.c
```

where file.c contains a statement of the form:

```
#include "regfile.i"
```

Once all the preprocessing is out of the way, the compiler *cc* and assembler *as* can be brought into play. As previously stated, these two invoke their own preprocessors *cpp* and *m4*. The output of these two processors are then compiled into object modules that are passed to the linkage editor (*ld*). Unless *ld* is told otherwise, the output of the linkage editor phase is stored in a file named *a.out*. Simple C-language programs can be compiled and tested easily:

```
cc file.s && a.out
cc file.c && a.out
```

More complex programs containing several modules must be compiled and then linked into an executable module. The linkage editor *ld* is automatically invoked by *cc* when needed:

```
cc file1.c file2.c file3.c file4.c -o ctest && ctest
```

In this example, all of the C files are compiled into their respective object files: file1.o, file2.o, file3.o, and file4.o. These are then linked together by *ld*, which is executed automatically by *cc*. The output of the linkage editor phase will be the executable program *test*.

For improved efficiency, the linkage editor or *strip* can be used to strip the symbol tables out of an executable program. The benefit of removing the symbol tables is that the programs load more quickly and require less disk space. The drawbacks are that the program cannot be easily debugged without the symbol tables and the executable program may not be portable between different releases of the UNIX operating system. Only final, production versions of programs should be stripped of their production tables.

Because the Shell scripts to accurately preprocess, compile, and link large programs would be overly complex, UNIX provides a command called *make* to handle the complexity of preprocessing, compiling, and linking programs. A prototype *makefile* is available in Appendix C.

Make recognizes all of the different file types in UNIX: SCCS (s.filename.c), C language (filename.c), Assembly language (filename.s), lex (filename.l), yacc (filename.y), object files (filename.o), and libraries (library.a). *Make,* for example, knows that to create an object file, it must first compile a C-language or assembly language file by the same name. It also knows that it may have to get the file from SCCS if it does not exist. *Make* decides what to do based on the last modification time of each file. If the object file is newer than either the SCCS or C-language file, *make* assumes that the object file is the most current and does not compile anything. If the SCCS file is newer, *make* gets the file from SCCS and compiles it to create the object module. The makefile to accomplish this task for a single source file would be as follows:

```
OBJECTS = cmdname.o              # name of the object file
cmdname: $(OBJECTS)              # command depends on cmdname.o
   cc $(OBJECTS) -o cmdname      # compile & link cmdname
```

Make automatically knows to look for the SCCS (s.cmdname.c) and source files (cmdname.c). Once a makefile is created, correctly compiling a program is as simple as:

```
make
```

The output from this command using the previous makefile would be:

```
get -p s.cmdname.c > cmdname.c
cc -c cmdname.c
cc cmdname.o -o cmdname
```

Since the date on s.cmdname.c was newer than either the C or object files, *make* executed *get* to retrieve the file from SCCS. Then, *make* executed the C compiler to create an object module (cmdname.o) from the source file. Finally, *make* executed the C compiler to link the object file into the executable program (cmdname).

Sometimes, a C-language file will include a data header file, filename.h, which may change and affect the resulting program. *Make* can know about these files and invoke the compiler when the header file changes:

```
OBJECTS = cmdname.o              # name of the object file
cmdname: $(OBJECTS)              # command depends on cmdname.o
   cc $(OBJECTS) -o cmdname      # compile & link cmdname
cmdname.o: cmdname.c cmdname.h
```

Similarly, a single program may depend on many object files. *Make* can be instructed, via the *makefile,* to compile all the modules and link them together:

```
OBJECTS = file1.o file2.o file3.o file4.o
cmdname: $(OBJECTS)              # command depends on all objects
   cc $(OBJECTS) -o cmdname      # compile & link the command
file1.o: file1.c file1.h         # object depends on header
```

This *makefile* will instruct *make* to compile all the objects, including file1.c, which also depends on file1.h. All four objects are created and then linked together. Since these larger compilations take longer to accomplish, the C-language programmer should put the whole process into background and continue working on other activities:

```
nohup nice make&
```

A listing of commands executed by *make* and the resulting errors will be stored in the file nohup.out for later examination.

Besides the variable, *OBJECTS,* there is another important *make* variable used to set the C compiler flags for all compiles and links: *CFLAGS*. This single variable can affect how all modules are compiled. To optimize the output of the compiler, for example, set CFLAGS to "-O":

```
CFLAGS = -O     # optimize executable code
```

Similarly, to include the regular expression and lexical analyzer libraries (PW and l) with the resulting executable program, set CFLAGS as follows:

```
CFLAGS = -O -lPW -ll     # optimize and include RE & LEX libs
```

To invoke the inclusion of test code defined in preprocessor statements, use CFLAGS to set the "-D" flag:

```
CFLAGS = -DTEST
```

which would cause the inclusion of code like the following:

```
#ifdef TEST
    fprintf(stderr,"Entering Main\n");
#endif
```

Using this technique, instruments can be left in the code to test its functioning, but turned on and off with the *make* variable CFLAGS.

In summary, UNIX comes with a variety of preprocessors, compilers, and a linkage editor that facilitate the construction of C-language programs. The Shell and *make* are both useful for executing these commands in the proper order to create executable programs. Once compiled, however, C-language programs must be tested and debugged.

4. TESTING AND DEBUGGING

The major UNIX commands that aid testing and debugging are shown in Figure 10.5. *Adb* and *sdb* are the two major debugging facilities. *Prof, time,* and *timex* are all useful for determining a program's efficiency. All these commands are useful for testing.

Adb, a debugger, is available with various versions of UNIX. *Sdb,* the symbolic debugger, is available with virtually all systems. When a program aborts or requires specialized testing, these debuggers can

```
adb    —a debugger
diff   —file comparison utility
dump   —dump object file
od     —octal dump
prof   —execution profiler
sdb    —symbolic debugger
time   —time commands
timex  —time commands and generate a system activity report
```

Figure 10.5 Testing and debugging commands.

analyze compiled C-language programs, *core* images of the program when it failed, and aid the programmer in analysis of the problem. To maximize the effectiveness of *sdb,* the program must be compiled with the "-g" option and the symbol table must not be stripped from the executable file:

cc -g *.c -o ctest && ctest ¦¦ sdb ctest

Or, the CFLAGS variable could have been changed to include the "-g" option and the program compiled and tested as follows:

make && ctest ¦¦ sdb ctest

This command stream will compile all C-language modules in the current directory, link them into a program called *ctest,* execute *ctest,* and if it fails, invoke *sdb.* Since most programs are compiled without the "-g" option or the symbol tables, this compilation and retest are required to generate all of the information needed by *sdb.*

A simple use of *sdb* traces the path the program took before ending abnormally. After executing *sdb* and receiving the *sdb* prompt (*), enter a lowercase *t:*

sdb ctest
*t
doprnt()
sub1()
main()

In this example, the program ended in *doprnt* (a printf function) and was called from *sub1. Sub1* was called from *main.* The C programmer can now trace potential paths of error in the subroutine *sub1.* To get a more specific trace, *ctest* would have to have been compiled with the "-g" option, but this example is sufficient for tracing most errors.

Sdb can also execute a program a line at a time allowing the programmer to watch its progress as it steps toward completion. *Adb* works much like *sdb.* Both of these facilities are useful when testing and debugging programs.

The three commands *prof, time,* and *timex,* can help identify programs that are resource hogs. *Time* and *timex* both give rudimentary indications that a program takes too many resources, either cpu or disk. *Prof* encourages a more exacting analysis of a program's efficiency. These three commands can be executed as follows:

time command

timex command

cc -p *.c -o command && command && prof command

The last command compiles the command with a "-p" option to invoke the creation the *mon.out* file readable by *prof.* The command is then executed and *prof* profiles the execution of the command using *mon.out.* The output of *prof* can be directed to a file, printer, or terminal as required. It can even be converted into graphical output:

prof -v command ¦ tplot -T4014

Each of these commands—*time, timex,* and *prof*—allows analysis of a program's execution in ways not possible with *sdb.* Once a program has executed, however, analysis focuses on the program's output.

The remaining commands—*diff* and *od*—help analyze the results of a program test. *Diff* compares files, while *od* generates an octal dump of a file. *Diff* is useful with standard files that end with a newline character (\n). *Od,* on the other hand, prints the unprintable, showing normally unreadable octal characters as their octal value. Because many terminals require control strings that may be unprintable, *od* provides a simple means to examine the output of commands that generate terminal control strings. Other files, like SCCS files, have embedded octal characters that cannot be detected without *od.* Both *diff* and *od* help analyze test results.

Diff, a file comparison utility, can examine two output files and display only those lines that differ. It shows which lines were added, changed, or deleted from the test output. This comparison aids a technique called regression testing—comparing the old to the new to ensure that only the desired changes occurred. Eliminating identical information from both tests helps the programmer determine the success or failure of a change:

```
oldcommand [args] > oldstdout 2>oldstderr
newcommand [args] > newstdout 2>newstderr
diff oldstdout newstdout ¦ pr
diff oldstderr newstderr ¦ pr
```

Examination of *diff's* output should indicate that the changes were made successfully or incorrectly.

Diff has several sister commands: *bdiff, sdiff,* and *sccsdiff. Bdiff* works on larger files than *diff* can handle. *Sdiff* gives a side-by-side difference listing, and *sccsdiff* compares two versions of an SCCS file. *Sccsdiff* is one of the best ways to determine the changes that occurred between two versions of a program's code, providing that the source code is stored in SCCS in the first place. SCCS is a major portion of the change control and configuration management facilities of UNIX.

5. CHANGE CONTROL AND CONFIGURATION MANAGEMENT

Change control and configuration management simply refer to the way that programs are built and changed in an orderly fashion. Working with UNIX and SCCS (Source Code Control System), you are fortunate to be working with one of the best tools available. SCCS stores C-language code, documents, shells, or anything consisting of text. The available SCCS commands are shown in Figure 10.6. When you are developing new shells or C-language programs and you complete an early working version, store the version in SCCS so that you can recover it later if required. When changing a program, retrieve the source code from SCCS, change it, store it, and then build the program from the SCCS source.

SCCS can hold all versions of a program, from infancy through adulthood, until it is scrapped. Most library systems will only hold the most current version of the source; the older versions are backed up on tape somewhere. Recovering old versions is no fun. With SCCS, how-

admin —add a file to SCCS
comb   —combine two versions of an SCCS file
delta —create a new version of an SCCS file
get   —get a file out of SCCS
prs   —print description of an SCCS file
rmdel —remove a delta from an SCCS file
sccsdiff—compare versions of an SCCS file
val   —validate an SCCS file
what   —look for *what* strings

Figure 10.6 SCCS commands for storing C-language code.

ever, it is simple. Even programmers on single-user systems will find SCCS of immeasurable value for controlling changes to software and documentation.

SCCS files can be kept in any directory, but for convenience it is best to store them in one location so that shells for accessing them can be built easily. Normally, they are stored under a directory called "sccs" which can exist under the user's home directory or the group's file system (see Figure 10.7). Some users prefer to store documentation with the program and others favor a separate directory. Once the organization of SCCS directories is decided, Shell interfaces to add or change SCCS files can be created easily.

The command to add files to SCCS is *admin*. It has a variety of options that are often unclear to new users. A simple Shell interface would accept the type of file, program name, and source name and add the file as follows:

```
#cadd program file
sccsdir = $HOME/sccs/C
if [ $# -eq 2 ]                    # two arguments?
then
    if [ ! -d $sccsdir/$program ]   # new program?
    then
        mkdir $sccsdir/$program     # create a directory
```

```
fi
    echo "Enter one line description"
    read desc
    admin -n -i$file -y"${desc}" $sccsdir/$program/s.$file
else
    echo "$0 syntax: $0 program file
fi
```

A user could add a program to SCCS easily with the following command and the code would be equally easy to retrieve:

cadd prg1 main.c

Similarly, to edit an SCCS file would require the following command:

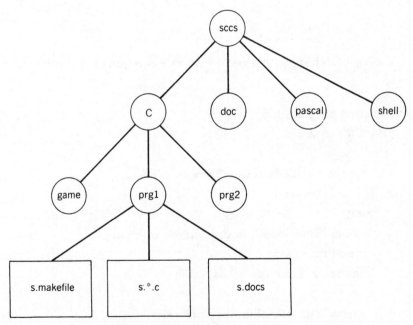

Figure 10.7 C-language SCCS directory structure.

```
#cedit program file
if [ $# -eq 2 ]
then
   sccsfile = $HOME/sccs/c/$program/s.$file
   if [ -r $sccsfile ]
   then
      get -e -s $sccsfile
      echo "$file has been retrieved for editing"
   else
      echo "File $sccsfile does not exist"
   fi
else
   echo "$0 syntax: $0 program file
fi
```

A user could retrieve the source as follows:

```
cedit prg1 main.c
```

To save the changed file back into SCCS requires a similar command:

```
#csave program file
if [ $# -eq 2 ]
then
   sccsfile = $HOME/sccs/c/$program/s.$file
   if [ -r $sccsfile ]
   then
      echo "Enter one line description of change"
      read comments
      delta -y"$comments" $sccsfile
   else
      echo "File $sccsfile does not exist"
   fi
```

```
else
    echo "$0 syntax: $0 type program file
fi
```

A user can save the changed source as follows:

```
csave prg1 main.c
```

SCCS also provides numerous ways to print information about SCCS files and the changes applied. *Prs* prints the status of various releases and levels of the source code. *Get* can retrieve the source code with the release and level number preceding each line of text. A simple command to print the history of changes to a file would be:

```
#chist program file
if [ $# -eq 2 ]
then
    sccsfile = $HOME/sccs/c/$program/s.$file
    if [ -r $sccsfile ]
    then
        prs -e -d":l: :D: :P: :C:" $sccsfile ¦ pr -h "$file"
    else
        echo "File $sccsfile does not exist"
    fi
else
    echo "$0 syntax: $0 program file
fi
```

Executing *chist* on an SCCS file would print a listing of changes (:I:), the dates the changes were created (:D:), the programmer who made the change (:P:), and the comments associated with the change (:D:). Reports of this type are useful to managers, analysts, and programmers for various activities.

Programmers, however, can get more out of a program listing containing the program code and the deltas associated with each line. A command similar to *chist* could be built to get this information:

get -p -m $sccsfile ¦ pr -o8 -h "Source listing for $file"

The output of this command would contain the SCCS release and level number from which each line was retrieved, a tab character, and then the source code line:

```
1.1   main(argc,argv)
1.1   int argc;
1.1   char **argv;
1.1   {
1.2   char c;
2.3   char *ptr;
```

Bugs are often found in recent modifications to the program. This facility of SCCS enables the programmer to quickly locate recent code changes. Managers can also track errors back to the release and level number of the source code.

The SCCS keywords (described in Chapter 7) can be used to automate version and run control in C-language programs. The version number of each C source file can be stored in a variable using the SCCS keyword "%A%":

static char *version = "%A%"; /* SCCS Version information */

When retrieved from SCCS, the keyword would expand to a *what* string that contains the source type, the source file name, and its release, level, branch, and sequence number:

static char *version = "@(#) clang filename.c 2.3.1.1 @(#)";

This information can be extracted from the *executable* program using *what* to check for proper version information:

what filename
clang filename.c 2.3.1.1

```
clang sub1.c 1.2
clang sub2.c 1.3.1.1
```

The version information can also be printed or written to run control files to log the execution of the command. The SCCS keywords give the programmer a strong tool for tracking and controlling change in C-language programs.

Other similar friendly interfaces to SCCS can be built around the remaining commands: *comb, rmdel, sccsdiff, val,* and *what.* The Shell can handle many functions that will not only improve change control and configuration management, but will also improve productivity and the quality of the resulting system. Many people, especially some of the UNIX gurus, question whether all this control is necessary, but as system complexities increase, the need for SCCS control becomes more intense.

6. SUMMARY

The Shell provides many tools that aid in the development and maintenance of C-language programs. The Shell can be used to develop working prototypes of C-language programs to test the correctness of their design. The Shell can be used to automate much of the coding, compiling, testing, and debugging processes. Even the control of changes to C-language source code, documentation, and other text files can be orchestrated by the Shell. Every development project needs a toolsmith to create these productivity tools. The examples in this chapter provide a starting point for further development and enhancement of the C-programming environment.

User friendly interfaces to all these commands can also be constructed to present the user with menus or windows into the C language. But the Shell can still automate most of the activities required during software development and maintenance. Use its facilities to maximize productivity and quality.

EXERCISES

1. Use the Shell to prototype a program that interactively prompts the user for his or her name, street address, city, and state. Put the output into a file for later use.

2. Use the Shell to prototype a program to select information from the /etc/passwd or /etc/group files. Format the output with *pr*.

3. Use *awk* to prototype a data selection and report program that selects the second, fourth, and fifth word from each input line and prints them in reverse order.

4. Write the statement to interactively compile and test the C-language prototype in Appendix B.

5. Use *admin* to create an SCCS file using the C-language prototype in Appendix B.

6. Use *get* to retrieve the file for editing.

7. Use *delta* to store the changed file back into SCCS.

8. Use *get* to retrieve the prototype from SCCS without the "-e" flag. What happened to all of the SCCS keywords?

CHAPTER

11

Working with Numbers

Every Shell programmer encounters the need to work with numbers: a sine here, a sum there, and an occasional graph. A significant part of UNIX is text, but the other part is numbers. Manipulating them and integrating them with the Shell is simple.

There are only a few commands that affect numbers: *bc, dc, expr, graphics, stat,* and *units. Graphics* encompasses all the commands that display numerical data in a graphical format. *Stat* is mentioned because it contains a library of mathematical functions. It can be found under *stat*(1) in the *UNIX User's Manual. Bc* and *dc* are basic and desk calculators that read the standard input and write on the standard output. *Expr* handles simple integer expressions like add, subtract, multiply, and divide. *Units* converts from one unit of measure to another. Any of these commands can help a Shell programmer manipulate numbers.

219

1. UNITS

Units is an interactive command, so it is not appropriate for inclusion in a Shell program. It can, however, provide the appropriate conversions for pounds to kilograms, feet to meters, miles per gallon to kilometers per liter, and miles per hour to furlongs per fortnight. The correct conversion is always at the user's command. The conversions can then be included in Shell commands as needed.

2. *EXPR*

Aside from handling various string comparisons and evaluations, *expr* also handles basic integer math: addition, subtraction, multiplication, and division. This facility is useful for simple mathematical processing and for controlling loops. Interactively, *expr* can handle simple calculations:

```
expr 327 + 431
758
expr 431 / 327
1
```

In loops, it can handle repetitious calculations. For example, the following command would sum all of the numbers from one to one hundred:

```
while [ ${i:= 1} -le 100 ]
do
   total = `expr ${total:=0} + ${i}`
   i = `expr ${i} + 1`
done
echo $total
```

Expr can also control the number of times a loop executes. Since the Bourne Shell has no *repeat* control construct, *expr* and *while* handle the repetition of processing.

```
while [ ${i:= 1} -le 10 ]        # repeat 10 times
do
    process something
    i='expr ${i} + 1'
done
```

The C Shell can handle simple integer arithmetic using standard C-language operators: $+$, $-$, $*$, $/$, and $\%$. When assigning values to parameters, the C Shell can use the integer operators of C: $+=$, $-=$, $*=$, $/=$, $++$, and $--$. The following example demonstrates the use of integer arithmetic:

```
if ( $variable + 1 > $maximum ) then
    @ var1 += 5
    @ var2--
endif
```

Handling more complex mathematics and floating point numbers requires the use of *bc* or *dc*.

3. BC AND DC

The desk calculator, *dc,* works just like a desk calculator, but is not as flexible as the basic calculator, *bc,* for use with Shell programs. *Bc,* using a syntax not unlike C or the C Shell, provides for unlimited precision arithmetic. It can also work in bases other than base 10. *Bc* has at its command the IF, FOR, and WHILE control structures. It also has access to various functions: sqrt, length, scale, sine, cosine, exponential, log, arctangent, and Bessel functions. *Bc* also allows users to define functions that can be included to handle complex math operations.

When executed, *bc* first reads any files that were specified as arguments. User defined functions can be stored in these files. Then, *bc* begins to read the standard input, which can be a file, a device, or a terminal. Two of the previous examples could be accomplished with *bc:*

```
echo "327 + 431" : bc              # add 327 and 431
758
echo "scale = 2;431 / 327" : bc    # divide 431 by 327
1.32
```

In the previous example, the *echo* command creates an input string for *bc*. The first example adds 327 and 431. The second example first sets the decimal accuracy (scale) to 2. Then, the division of 431 by 327 is echoed into *bc*. Unless set to another value, the *scale* of every *bc* command defaults to zero decimal places.

For simple integer arithmetic, *expr* is the best choice. But when higher precision is required, *bc* handles the job nicely.

Bc can also use the math library functions to calculate various limited equations. To calculate the sine of all angles from 1° to 90°, the basic calculator can be invoked in a *while* loop:

```
while [ ${angle:=1} -le 90 ]       # for angles <= 90
do
   # calculate the sine to four decimal places
   sin=`echo "scale 4;s(${angle})" : bc -l`
   echo "Angle=${angle} Sine=${sin}"     # print the result
   i=`expr ${angle} + 1`                  # increment the angle
done
```

Bc can also handle functions stored in files to process more complex equations. The following functions handle converting degrees Fahrenheit to degrees Celsius:

```
scale=2
define f(c) {              /* convert celsius to fahrenheit */
   auto f                  /* fahrenheit variable */
   f = ( c * 1.8 ) + 32    /* convert */
   return(f)               /* return value */
}
define c(f) {              /* convert fahrenheit to celsius */
   auto c                  /* celsius variable */
```

```
    c = ( f − 32 ) / 1.8      /* convert */
    return(c)                 /* return value */
}
```

Assuming that these functions were contained in a file called temp, conversions could be handled by invoking *bc:*

```
bc temp        # invoke bc with fahrenheit/celsius conversions
f(100)         # convert 100 degrees celsius to fahrenheit
212.00
c(32)          # convert 32 degrees fahrenheit to celsius
0.00
quit
```

Or the results could be stored in a variable:

```
fahrenheit = `echo "f(100)" ¦ bc temp`
celsius = `echo "c(0)" ¦ bc temp`
```

Although these are simple examples, *bc* can use functions to process significantly more complex arithmetic equations as the need arises. *Bc* can also handle other functions required by programmers, like conversion of numbers from one base into another.

Computers use base 2 for their calculations, but most of them display their information in octal (base 8) or hexadecimal (base 16). *Bc* can handle these conversions easily by assigning an input base and/or an output base. An octal calculator would set both input base (*ibase*) and output base (*obase*) to 8:

```
bc
ibase = 8      /* set input base to octal */
obase = 8      /* set output base to octal */
11 + 7         /* octal 11 + 7 = 20 octal */
20
quit
```

The same facility is available for the hexadecimal environment. Or hexadecimal or octal can be converted directly to decimal:

```
bc
ibase = 8      /* input base is octal, output base is decimal /*
10             /* octal 10 is 8 decimal */
8
ibase = 16     /* input base is hexadecimal output base is decimal */
10             /* hexadecimal 10 is 16 decimal */
16
quit
```

In the previous example, an octal 10 is equal to a decimal 8 and a hexadecimal 10 is equal to a decimal 16. When reading octal or hexadecimal dumps of data or programs, these calculators can improve any programmer's productivity.

When expressions or statistics are required that are more complex than those provided by *bc*, the statistics library, *stat,* can be used to handle more difficult mathematics.

4. STAT

All of the statistical analysis tools are available under /usr/bin/graf. Any system that does not have the graphics subsystem will miss these tools. To have access to these tools, the PATH variable should be modified to include /usr/bin/graf. An interactive user can enter the command *graphics* to add the bin to their PATH:

```
$ graphics
^
```

The *graphics* command gives a different prompt "^" to let the user know that they are connected to the graphics subsystem.

The statistics filters available in *stat* are shown in Figure 11.1. Most of them accept numbers from the standard input. Each number on the

abs   —absolute value
af   —arithmetic function
bucket —summarize into buckets
ceil   —round up to next integer
cor   —calculate correlation coefficient
cusum   —cumulative summary
exp   —exponential
floor   —round down to next integer
gamma   —gamma function
hilo   —get high or low value
list   —list input
log   —logarithmic function
lreg   —linear regression analysis
mean   —calculate mean
mod   —calculate modulus
power   —raise to a power
prod   —calculate internal product
qsort   —quick sort the input
rank   —rank the input
root   —calculate any root
round   —round to the nearest integer
sin   —sine
total   —total the input
var   —calculate the variance of the input

Figure 11.1   Statistical commands contained in *stat*.

standard input, whether it comes from a file or a command or a device, is a separate input to the command.

A command to extract the previous 12 months' worth of data and calculate the total, mean, and variance of the data would be:

```
tail -12 file > /tmp/tmp$$          # get last 12 entries
yearsum = `total < /tmp/tmp$$`      # total 12 entries
```

```
yearmean = `mean < /tmp/tmp$$`       # get mean of 12 entries
yearvar = `var < /tmp/tmp$$`         # calculate variance
echo "Sum = $yearsum, Mean = $yearmean, Variance = $yearvar."
```

All the *stat* functions can be used in this way to answer most numerical processing requirements. The output of many of these commands serves as input to the graphical commands described in the next section.

The number generators shown in Figure 11.2 can develop test data for commands or drive the graphical commands described in the next section. To generate a sequence of integers from 1 to 10, *gas* is invoked:

```
gas -s1 -t10
  1     2     3     4     5
  6     7     8     9     10
```

To generate a random number based on today's date as a seed number:

```
rand -n1 -s`date `+%j`
```

Or based on the second:

```
rand -n1 -s`date '+%S'`
```

Stat's generators and summarizers each enhance a Shell user's ability to deal with numbers. The remaining commands of interest display numerical data in graphical format.

```
gas    —generate a sequence of numbers
prime—generate a sequence of prime numbers
rand   —generate a random sequence of numbers
```

Figure 11.2 Number generators.

5. GRAPHICS

The UNIX graphics subsystem, as it has existed since Version 3, is not as robust as most of the microcomputer graphics systems. In many ways, it is one of the most unfriendly subsystems of UNIX. But once numbers have been manipulated into a format that facilitates plots and graphs, a number of commands can be used to display them graphically. I expect that AT&T or Berkeley will move quickly to provide filters for Hewlett-Packard plotters and color microcomputer monitors. I also expect that these filters will have a better user interface than the current package.

Assuming that a UNIX user will need graphics is like saying that a picture is worth a thousand words. The shells required to plot graphs are simple to build and use. The following sections describe how to use the Shell and the graphics commands shown in Figure 11.3 to create most forms of graphical output.

UNIX also contains a graphical editor and a variety of input and output filters (Figure 11.4). These commands and their applications are also discussed.

5.1. Types of Graphics

There are bar charts, pie charts, histograms, straight-line plots, smooth-line plots, and painted graphics. The standard UNIX graphics package can handle most charts and plots, but does not fare as well with painted graphics. Anyone who has seen the capabilities of Apple's MacIntosh or PC Paint will quickly agree. But AT&T cannot be far

bar   —draw a bar chart
hist —draw a histogram
pie   —draw a pie chart
plot —plot a graph
label—label the X or Y axis of a graph
title —title a graph

Figure 11.3   Chart and plot commands.

dtoc   —directory table of contents

erase   —erase a 4114 screen

ged   —graphical editor

graph   —draw a graph

graphics —includes graphics commands in PATH

gtop   —graphics to plot filter

hardcopy—print Tektronix 4114 screen

hpd   —HP 7221 plotter filter

ptog   —plot to graphics filter

spline   —interpolates smooth curves

td   —Tektronix 4114 display

tplot   —graphics filters for Diablo and Tektronix terminals

ttoc   —text table of contents

vtoc   —visual table of contents

whatis   —help for graphics commands

Figure 11.4 Graphics commands.

behind. UNIX is widely used for graphics applications like computer aided design (CAD) and computer-aided manufacturing (CAM). Some computer-aided programming (CAP) packages are also available. But only a subset of these packages are included in standard UNIX.

The major programming oriented graphics facility is *vtoc:* a visual table of contents or, as it is more commonly known, a hierarchy chart. Using text files like the following one, *vtoc* can create a hierarchy chart for display on a Tektronix graphics terminal or other graphical output device:

```
0. main.c
1. loadtbl.c
2. drawhier.c
2.1. box.c
2.2. text.c

vtoc -cdi hierarchy ¦ td               # Tektronix display
vtoc -cdi hierarchy ¦ gtop ¦ tplot -T450    # Diablo display
```

Project managers use Gant charts and critical path analysis that are not currently available in the UNIX graphics package. A number of UNIX project management packages provide these capabilities, however.

Each of the major plotting commands—*bar, hist, pie,* and *plot*—expects input in the form of a sequence of numbers (known in the math world as a vector) and produce a GPS (graphical primitive string) as output. A GPS compresses the format of a graphical file. The resulting file can be edited and displayed by UNIX commands like *ged* and *td.* A GPS can be displayed on a Tektronix terminal with *td* or converted to *tplot* input using *gtop. Tplot* input is only a series of points to plot. It does not use the GPS format. *Graph* and *spline* expect pairs of numbers as input and produce pairs of X and Y coordinates as output. These coordinate pairs can be plotted using *tplot* or converted to a GPS using *ptog.*

Title can be used to add a title to a vector (especially useful with *plot*) or to add a title to a GPS. *Label* puts labels on the X or Y axis of the *bar, hist,* or *plot* graphs. All of these commands can be combined to produce useful graphs.

5.2. Bar Charts and Histograms

Bar charts and histograms are a snap once you have files of numbers and matching descriptions to be used as labels:

```
inputfile
1      2      3      4      5      6      7      8

labelfile
Jan    Feb    Mar    Apr    May    Jun    Jul    Aug

bar -g,xa inputfile : label -c,-r-45,Flabelfile,p,x : \
    title -c,l"Lower Title",u"Upper Title" : td
```

This example accepts data from the inputfile and creates a bar graph GPS that eliminates the grid (-g) and X-axis labels (-xa). The output of the *bar* command is labeled on the X-axis using the labelfile.

Each label is rotated (-r-45) a negative 45° from horizontal. This output is then given upper and lower titles. The end result of this entire process is displayed using the Tektronix display command *td*.

Hist could have been substituted for *bar* to obtain a histogram. The Tektronics display (*td*) could be changed to *gtop* to display the output on a Diablo printer:

```
bar -g,xa inputfile : label -c,-r-45,Flabelfile,p,x : \
   title -c,l"Lower Title",u"Upper Title" : \
   gtop : tplot -T450
```

5.3.   Pie Charts

Pie charts are not significantly different from bar charts. Labels for each slice of the pie are kept in the input file instead of in a separate file. To put the previous example files together and create a pie chart is simple:

```
paste inputfile labelfile > piefile
pie piefile : title -c,l"Lower Title",u"Upper Title" : td
```

For more information on how to use *pie,* or any of the graphics commands for that matter, ask the system *whatis pie. Whatis* is the graphical help command.

5.4.   Plots

Plots can use a single vector (file of numbers) or several as input. *Plot* just connects the dots. Each vector plotted is represented by a different line: solid, dotted, dot dashed, dashed, and so on. Each vector can have a title that will be displayed along the Y axis. Creating a line plot can be accomplished as follows:

```
title -c,v"Vector title" inputfile : \
   plot -g,xa : label -c,-r-45,Flabelfile,p,x : \
      title -c,l"Lower Title",u"Upper Title" : td
```

In this example, the inputfile is given a title that will be printed along the Y axis. The output is plotted, suppressing the grid and X-axis labels. The plot is then labeled and titled before being displayed with *td*.

5.5. *Graph* and *Spline*

Both *graph* and *spline* accept pairs of X and Y coordinates as input. Their output is especially suited to use with *tplot*. They are useful for generating simple plots on a Diablo printer:

```
graph < inputfile ¦ tplot -T450
spline < inputfile ¦ tplot -T450
```

Their output can also be converted for use with *label, title,* and *td:*

```
graph < inputfile ¦ ptog ¦ label -c,-r-45,Flabelfile,p,x ¦ \
    title -c,l"Lower Title",u"Upper Title" ¦ td
```

In this example, *graph* plots the X and Y coordinates in the input file. The output is converted from plot to GPS format with *ptog*. The result is labeled and titled before the graph is displayed on a Tektronix terminal.

Although somewhat complex, these commands can meet most of a UNIX user's graphics needs.

6. SUMMARY

The UNIX Shell offers a wide variety of commands to manipulate numbers and calculate statistics. The basic calculator (*bc*), Shell expression evaluator (*expr*), statistics library (*stat*), graphics commands, and units conversion program (*units*) each provide the tools necessary to handle most of the arithmetic requirements of a typical Shell user.

Because of their ability to work with standard input and output, *bc, expr, graphics,* and *stat* can be used directly in Shell programs. *Units* can only be used interactively. Everything from simple integer addition to linear regression analysis can be performed with these tools. Numerical analysis was never easier.

EXERCISES

1. Calculate Pi (22/7) using *expr* and *bc*. Calculate Pi to four decimal places using *bc*.

2. Use *expr* to add all of the numbers from 1 to 100.

3. Use *bc* to calculate the log, l(n), of the numbers from 1 to 10. Use *bc* to calculate the natural log (l(n)/l(2)) of the same numbers.

4. Create a function to handle the natural log calculation in the previous exercise.

5. Use *bc* to convert decimal numbers into octal and hexadecimal. Convert octal numbers to hexadecimal.

6. Generate a hierarchy chart using any program of interest.

7. Generate a *bar, hist, pie,* and *plot* graph of the numbers from 1 to 10.

12

UNIX System Administration

A well-administered UNIX system is a joy to both the administrator and the system's users. The key to proper system administration is the Shell.

Shell programs can automate most of the activities of the system's administration and operations staff. Automating activities like adding users or backing up the file systems help ensure that nothing is forgotten or done incorrectly. Even the best typists (which UNIX administrators are not) have a hard time entering the complete command to *volcopy* a disk to a backup disk or tape without errors. Since file system backups are often done at night when even the best console operators are not totally awake, errors can occur unless the system does most of the work for them.

Other administration activities require no human intervention at all. These can be automated with Shell and executed as required by *cron,* the clock daemon that executes commands based on the system's internal clock.

This chapter covers how the Shell can automate many of the system administrator's activities, the files used for system administration, operational shells, and restricted shells. Because of its ability to handle complex processes reliably, the Shell is the key to productive, high-quality system administration.

1.   ADMINISTRATIVE DIRECTORIES AND FILES

A UNIX system administrator is directly involved with the directories shown in Figure 12.1. Each directory contains files and commands that affect system administration.

The major files and commands of concern to the system administrator are shown in Figures 12.2 and 12.3. The file system, /etc, contains most of the commands required for system operation.

The UNIX system administrator is also responsible for the Shell

/etc	—administrative and operational commands reside here as well as password and group files
/usr/adm	—accounting directories
/usr/docs	—system documentation
/usr/games	—games
/usr/lib	—operational logs, cron tables, commands
/usr/lib/acct	—accounting commands
/usr/lib/uucp	—UUCP commands
/usr/lp	—line printer spooling system
/usr/news	—local news directory
/usr/pub	—public directories
/usr/rje	—Remote Job Entry system
/usr/spool	—spooling directories
/usr/spool/lp	—line printer spooling directory
/usr/spool/uucp	—UNIX to UNIX communications directory
/usr/tmp	—temporary directories

Figure 12.1   Administrative directories.

```
/etc
    /etc/brc           —executed at startup by init
    /etc/checklist     —default file systems checked by fsck
    /etc/group         —listing of group IDs
    /etc/inittab       —event list for init
    /etc/motd          —message of the day
    /etc/mnttbl        —list of mounted file systems
    /etc/passwd        —login list and password file
    /etc/profile       —custom shell executed by login
    /etc/rc            —startup shell executed by init
    /etc/termcap       —terminal capabilities database
    /etc/wtmp          —log of login processes
/usr/adm
    /usr/adm/pacct —accounting log
/usr/lib
    /usr/lib/cronlog—log of cron processing
    /usr/lib/crontab—event list for cron
```

Figure 12.2 Administrative files.

and C commands that are locally developed. The source code, as well as the commands themselves, should be maintained on one system and then delivered to any other systems. Shell can help automate building and delivering locally developed software to other systems. Once received, the other systems can automatically install the software in the appropriate *bin* directories.

The other files that a system administrator deals with are not really files at all, but devices—terminals, disks, tapes, and line printers—that handle special functions in a UNIX system. These are known as special files and come in two varieties: character and block special. The various block and special files are shown in Figure 12.4. They are all created with the *mknod* command when the system is installed.

Shell commands write to character special files directly, while block special files require special commands. Character special files act just like regular files. The following examples echo the system date onto

/etc

config	—configure a UNIX system
crash	—crash the system
cron	—execute commands in /usr/lib/crontab
diskbackup	—backup file systems to disk
doff	—stop block special file
don	—start block special file
dskfmt	—format a disk pack
fsck	—check a file system's validity
fsdb	—debug file system errors
init	—initialize system for operation
killall	—kill all processes
labelit	—label a disk or tape volume
mkfs	—make a file system
mknod	—make a special file node
mount	—mount a file system
shutdown	—gracefully shut the system down
startup	—gracefully start it up
tapebackup	—backup file systems to tape
umount	—umount a file system
volcopy	—volcopy a file system
wall	—send a message to all users logged in

Figure 12.3   Administrative commands in /etc.

the console, copy the contents of a directory to a tape, and print a file on the line printer:

```
date > /dev/console       # print date on console
find . -cpio /dev/rmt0    # backup a directory to tape
pr file > /dev/lp1        # print a file on a line printer
```

Special files can also be restricted with *chmod* to prevent users from writing to them. For example, terminals (/dev/tty) should be mode 700 to prevent other users from writing directly onto their terminals while they are working. Only /etc/wall overrides this protection.

/dev   Block and Character Special Files

Block Devices
    dsk*   —3B20 disks
    mt*   —tape drives
    rp*   —DEC disks

Character Devices
    acu   —auto call unit
    console—system console
    rdsk   —3B20 disks
    rmt*   —tape drives
    rrp*   —DEC disks
    lp   —line printer
    tty   —terminals
    vpm   —virtual protocol machines (RJE)

Figure 12.4   Block and character special devices.

Most of the block and character special files are the province of the system administrator. They facilitate disk and tape backups, console messages, terminal communications, and so on. Administrators will gain the most familiarity with their use and benefits when used in the Shell.

Aside from locally developed commands and special files, the administrative files, commands, and directories can be broken into several categories: daily administration, automated administration, system start-up, and system shutdown. Each of the following sections covers the application of the Shell to these activities.

2. DAILY ADMINISTRATION

Hardly a day goes by when the administrator is not asked to add or delete a user or group from the system, restore a file, or inform the users of changes in commands, operations, or whatever. Each activity represents various levels of effort required of the system administrator. Possibly the most frequent activity required is the addition of a user.

Adding a user is not as simple as it sounds. Entries must be made in the passwd and group files. Directories and files must be created. Environment variables must be established to point the user's login toward correct line printers, RJE lines, and so on. Because remembering all of these things is impossible and means that the administrator could never take a vacation, it makes sense to automate this activity with the Shell. To add a user, the passwd file must be updated first:

```
# get last user no
usrno = `tail -1 /etc/passwd ¦ cut -f3 -d:`
usrno = `expr $usrno + 1`                    # increment user no
echo "Which group will user belong to?"
read group                                   # get group number
grpno = `grep $group /etc/group ¦ cut -f3 -d:`
echo "User's login name?"
read logname
echo "User's name and phone?"
read usrname
echo "File system?"
read fs
echo "${logname}:...,:${usrno}:${grpno}:${usrname}:/${fs}/${logname}: \
    /bin/sh" >> /etc/passwd                  # add user entry to password file
```

Next, *adduser* will have to create the user's directories and files:

```
homedir = /${fs}/${logname}
mkdir ${homedir}                    # make login directory
mkdir ${homedir}/bin               # make other required directories
mkdir ${homedir}/doc
mkdir ${homedir}/rje
mkdir ${homedir}/src
# add profile
cp /unixfs/proto/profile ${homedir}/.profile
```

```
# all dirs readable
chmod 755 ${homedir} ${homedir}/*
# writable
chmod 777 ${homedir}/src ${homedir}/rje
chmod 700 ${homedir}/.profile      # unchangeable
#
# make all files and directories owned by user & group
#
chown ${logname} ${homedir} ${homedir}/* ${homedir}/.profile
chgrp ${group} ${homedir} ${homedir}/* ${homedir}/.profile
```

These few Shell commands comprise the basic needs of the *adduser* command. As the user population requires more hooks into the additional subsystems of UNIX (*lp*, *rje*, etc.), the *adduser* command should be enhanced to establish all the environmental variables required to make the user's entrance into the system as comfortable as possible. Taking care of all of these details when adding a user to a system not only helps the user, but keeps the administrator from having to answer numerous phone calls from frustrated users.

The command to add a group to the /etc/group file would be similar in format to *adduser*. *Addgroup* can be created easily with a few modifications to the commands shown.

Another frequently required procedure deletes users. To delete a user, all references to the user must be removed from the system including /etc/passwd, /etc/group, and /fs/logname. Using the same variable names as used in *adduser*, *deluser* executes as follows:

```
# deluser - remove /etc/passwd entry
sed -e "/^${logname}/d" < /etc/passwd > /etc/opasswd
cp /etc/opasswd /etc/passwd      # replace passwd file
ed /etc/group <<!                # remove group entry
g/${logname},/s///
g/,${logname}/s///
w
q
!
```

```
cd /${fs}/${logname}            # change dir to user directory
if [ $? -eq 0 ]                 # successful cd?
then
    rm -rf *                    # remove all files and directories
    cd ..
    rmdir ${logname}            # remove user directory
else
    echo "OOPS -- /${fs}/${logname} not found"
fi
```

Again, as more hooks are added to a system's users, *deluser* will
need to delete more references to the login name. Aside from administering logins, the system administrator must restore files and directories when a user inadvertently removes a semiprecious file. Note
that this is less likely to happen in a C Shell system when the user has
the *noclobber* variable set.

Restoring files requires that the operations staff mount the correct
backup disk. What better way to ensure that the most current backup
copy is used than to let the Shell request the backup disk from a
history log? Assuming that the disk backup command creates a log of
the file systems backed up and the volume names of the backup disks, a
command called *filerestore* could determine which disk to use:

```
# filerestore
echo "Enter full path name: /fs/userid/dir.../filename"
read path
fs = `echo $path ! cut -f2 -d"/"`
backup = `grep $fs /etc/backuplog ! tail -1`      # get latest log
backupvol = `echo ${backup} ! cut -f2 -d:`        # get volume
special = `echo ${backup} ! cut -f3 -d:`          # get special name
echo "Mount $backupvol on backup drive"
echo "Hit <return> key when ready to continue"
read answer
mount ${special} /bck                             # mount backup as bck
file = `echo $path ! cut -f3- -d/`                # cut filesys from path
```

```
cp /bck/${file} $path                          # copy backup file
umount ${special}                              # unmount backup drive
echo "${path} restored from /bck/${file}"
echo "Remove $backupvol from backup drive"
```

If the backup log contained the following information:

```
unix1:bkuptues:/dev/rdsk140
unix2:bkuptues:/dev/rdsk142
unix1:bkupwed:/dev/rdsk140
unix2:bkupwed:/dev/rdsk142
```

then the command to back up the file, /unix1/lja/src/main.c, would ask the system administrator to mount the disk labeled bkupwed on the backup drive (in this case dsk14). The *filerestore* command would then mount the backup file system as /bck and copy the previous version of the file into the requested directory and file.

For users on System V, the backup disks must be brought on-line using *don* and *doff*. Modify *filerestore* to use these System V commands. Another frequent requirement calls for the restoration of entire directories or file systems from disk or tape. I leave it to the reader to enhance *filerestore* to handle more complex restorations.

The final requirement of daily administration is the communication of all system changes to the user population. A knowledgeable user population minimizes the number of phone calls an administrator will receive. The commands that handle user communication are *mail, news,* and *wall.* The file *motd,* message of the day, can also be used to provide daily information when the user logs into UNIX. The following example shows various entries for *motd:*

/etc/motd
The system will be down for preventive maintenance Sunday, July 17 from 9A.M. to 6P.M. Please refer questions to x1234.

News is used for changes to the system or system commands. Users can read the daily news when they have time. News files are kept in the directory /usr/news. *Mail* communicates directly with specific users or groups of users. *Wall* writes to all users who are logged in when immediate communication is required (i.e., when the system is coming down for emergency maintenance).

Shell programming can aid the system administrator in all phases of daily administration. Shell commands should be developed to automate any activity that happens frequently (e.g., adding or deleting users, or restoring files). Other administrative tasks must occur on a set schedule. Rather than demand that these be done by the administrator, they can be executed automatically by *cron*.

3.   CRON

Cron reads /usr/lib/crontab and executes the commands found according to the time specifications. *Cron* gives the system administrator a handy way of being everywhere, doing everything, without having to be on the system.

Crontab entries have six fields. The first five fields tell *cron* when to execute the command: minute (0–59), hour (0–23), day (1–31), month (1–12), and day of the week (0–6, Sunday = 0 and Saturday = 6). To match a number of different times or days, a field may contain numbers separated by commas. To match any time or day, an asterisk (*) can be used in any of these fields. The sixth field contains the command to be executed.

A simple crontab will have entries to print the date and time on the console every 30 minutes and to *sync* the super block every 10:

```
0,30 * * * * date > /dev/console; echo "\n" > /dev/console
0,10,20,30,40,50 * * * * /bin/sync > /dev/null
```

To execute the *calendar* program every weekday morning at 5 A.M., add the following line to /usr/lib/crontab:

```
0 5 * * 1-5 /usr/bin/calendar -
```

The system administrator should use *cron* to handle as many routine tasks as possible. These include activities such as monitoring disk usage, cleaning up temporary files, validating SCCS files, keeping system logs to a reasonable size, printing accounting reports, or administering subsystems like *lp* and *rje*. The system can handle all kinds of detective work in non-prime-time hours when the administrator is home having dinner or sleeping. Use *cron* like an army of administrators and have it send detected errors to the real administrator for resolution.

Cron is started when the system is brought up and stops when the system is shut down for backups. Both of these activities—startup and shutdown—can be automated with the Shell to further reduce operational costs and errors.

4. STARTUP

Starting the system is handled by *init*. When the system is brought up from the console, it is in single-user mode: init 1; /etc/inittab controls the actions of *init* in each of its states. In the single-user mode, it executes *brc*. Users of System V will have to make the disks available to the system using *don* and then execute *init* 2, which executes /etc/rc and brings all the terminal devices (/dev/tty) on line.

The command /etc/rc should check all the file systems for errors using fsck, mount the file systems, and start the process accounting, cron, the RJE, *lp, uucp,* and anything else that should be available when users enter the system.

Since /etc/brc and /etc/rc are shells, they can be modified to ensure that the system comes up cleanly, ready for users. Each file can execute special shells to handle the requirements of the system administrator, like mailing the date and time of system startup. All these files /etc/inittab, /etc/brc, and /etc/rc are under the control of the system administrator and should evolve to simplify system operation.

5. SHUTDOWN

How the system is shut down is probably more important than how it is started. Rash actions like halting the machine before all commands are killed, file systems unmounted, accounting stopped, subsystems stopped, and so on can generate many problems that could be avoided by using the *shutdown* command. Since *shutdown* is a Shell command, it can be modified to improve system reliability.

Once the system has been shut down gracefully, placed in single-user mode, and had its file systems checked, the *shutdown* command should ask the operator about disk or tape backups and execute these commands as required. A system administrator can reduce the possibility of lost files by requiring nightly backups and by automating the backup process with Shell commands to mount the proper backup disk or tape and *volcopy* the file systems.

The disk and tape backup commands are similar. The following command will backup the *root* and *usr* file systems:

```
# diskbackup
day = `date + %a`              # get day of week Sun-Sat
echo "Backup volume name is bck${day}
doff mhd 14 > /dev/null        # unmount backup drive
echo "Mount backup pack labeled FILE SYSTEM = root"
echo "Hit return when ready"
read answer
don mhd 14 > /dev/null         # mount root backup
volcopy root /dev/rdsk0 unix0 /dev/rdsk140 bck${day}
volcopy usr /dev/rdsk2 unix0 /dev/rdsk142 bck${day}
doff mhd 14 > /dev/null        # unmount backup drive
```

The command could also use *labelit* to check the volume name of the backup pack before continuing. Disk and tape backup commands should be developed for each system to ensure the accuracy of the backup procedures. There is nothing more vicious than a user who has lost data and work. Do not let this happen to your system's users.

6.   ADMINISTRATIVE SHELLS

Nothing is more frustrating to a UNIX user than to need help and not know where to call to get it. Consider building a simple command, called *helpme,* that prints the administrator's work and home phone numbers. If there is more than one administrator and each specializes in certain UNIX subsystems, then include that information, too:

```
# helpme
cat /global/help/oncall      # print list of administrators
```

Periodically check all the system logs for signs of trouble. As certain kinds of errors rise to the surface, develop Shell commands to *grep* for errors in the logs and mail them to the system administrator nightly using *cron*. The sooner errors are detected and corrected, the sooner the administrator can kick back and spend his or her time developing new and better tools to support the user population.

7. RESTRICTED SHELLS

Occasionally, the administrator will need to allow a group of users access to the machine without giving them all of the power of UNIX. In these instances, the system administrator can create a restricted environment that lets them perform some necessary work, but prohibits them from going crazy in the system. Creating restricted Shells is easy.

First, the administrator creates a restricted login that points to /bin/rsh instead of /bin/sh. Upon login, the user is prohibited from executing the *cd* command, changing the value of PATH, redirecting output, or executing commands beginning with "/". These restrictions are enforced only after *login* has executed the commands in the user's .profile.

By creating the proper .profile and not allowing the user to change it, the system administrator can put the restricted user in any directory, supply any commands required with PATH, and rest assured that he or she can do little damage.

The commands required are often linked from /bin and /usr/bin to a set of restricted bins: /rbin and /usr/rbin. A simple .profile to restrict a user's activities would be:

```
PATH = :/rbin:/usr/rbin
cd /unixfs/rdir
export PATH
```

The user could then execute the commands in the current directory, /rbin, and /usr/rbin, but would be restricted from moving about the system. This is only useful, occasionally, but it is an option for good system administration. Use restricted shells sparingly; users should be free to optimize their use of UNIX.

8. SUMMARY

The UNIX system administrator has as much to gain from Shell usage as any UNIX user. Much of the work of administering a system can be handled with Shell commands, *cron,* and the startup and shutdown procedures. Productive UNIX usage relies on extensive use of the Shell and all its facilities. From the UNIX guru to the simplest user, Shell is the way to keep a user from working too hard to accomplish his or her goals.

As I mentioned in the Preface, watching an IBM COBOL programmer do anything is like watching a man try to kick a whale across a beach with his bare feet. Some people feel that UNIX is equally difficult, but they have not developed an understanding of the Shell and how to make it work for them. May you spend your time collecting rare and beautiful shells to satisfy your every need.

EXERCISES

1. Write the command to allow users to create news files in /usr/news.

2. Write the command to send mail to groups of users by extracting their user IDs from the /etc/group file.

3. Write the command to backup file systems to tape on your system. (Look up your device types for magnetic tape.)

4. Write the commands to restore files and file systems from tape.

5. Modify the backup command to include all the disks and file systems on your UNIX system.

6. Write the crontab entry to print the accounting reports in /usr/adm/acct/fiscal on a line printer.

7. Write the crontab entry to validate all of the SCCS files on the system and send mail of the corrupted files to the system administrator.

Bibliography

AT&T, *The Bell System Technical Journal*, Vol. 57, No. 6, Part 2, 1978.

Bell Laboratories, *UNIX User's Manual*, Release 3.0, June 1980.

Bell Laboratories, *UNIX User's Manual*, Release 4.1, June 1981.

Bell Laboratories, *UNIX User's Manual*, Release 5.0, June 1983.

Stevens, W. P., How Data Flow Can Improve Application Development Productivity, *IBM Syst. J.*, **21**(2), 1982.

A

Reusable Shell Code

```
#
#           %M% %Y% %I%
#
#              Most recent update: %G% at %U%
#
#%Z% Function -
#%Z%
#
#@#@ Syntax -
#
#%Z% General Instructions -
#%Z%
#%Z% Parameters -
#%Z%     Required -
```

```
#%Z%
#%Z%    Optional -
#%Z%
#   store the flags
while [ `echo $1 : cut -f1` = "-" ]
do
    parms="${parms} $1"
    shift
done
case $# in
    #      if they don't give any files, prompt for them
    0)
        echo "enter filename"
        read filename
        ;;
    #      if they give exactly the right number, do something
    1)
        filename=$1
        ;;
    #      if they give a whole bunch, process all of them
    *)
        filename="$*"
        ;;
esac
#describe actual processing
for file in ${filename}
do
    process $file
done
```

B

C-Language Prototype

```
char mainrel [] = "%A%"; /* SCCS keywords */
#include <stdio.h>
#include <string.h>
main(argc, argv)
int argc;
char **argv;
{
    /***************************************
    *                                     *
    *   main program:                     *
    *                                     *
    *   program description:              *
    *                                     *
    *   subroutines called or required:   *
    *                                     *
    *   reference:                        *
    *                                     *
    *            %A%                       *
    *                                     *
    **************************************
    */
```

```
char *cmdname;
    cmdname = argv[0];        /* save pointer to the commandname */
    argc--; argv++;           /* increment argument pointers */
    /*
        check for control flags
    */
    while (argc>1 && *argv[0] = = '-') {
        switch(argv[0][1]) {
        case 'f':      /* flags */
                       /* insert flag processing */
            break;
        default:
            fprintf(stderr, "%s: invalid parameter %s\n",
                cmdname, argv[0]);
            exit(1);
            break;
        }      /* END SWITCH */
        argc--;          /* decrement the argument counter */
        argv++;          /* increment the argument pointer */
    }      /* END WHILE */
    if (argc < 1) {   /* oops, no files */
        fprintf(stderr, "%s syntax: %s -[flags] file(s)",
            cmdname, cmdname);
        exit(1);
    } else {        /* process files in argument list */
      while(argc>0) {
        if (freopen(argv[0], "r", stdin) = = NULL) {
            fprintf(stderr,"%s: can't open %s\n", cmdname, file);
            exit(1);
        } else {
          /* process input file */
        }      /* END IF */
```

```
        argc--; argv++;
    }     /* END WHILE */
  }     /* END IF */
}     /* END MAIN */
```

C

Makefile Prototype

```
OBJECTS = main.o sub.o lex.yy.o y.tab.o
LIB = -lm
CFLAGS = -O
BIN = /unixfs/bin
command: $(OBJECTS)
        cc $(CFLAGS) $(OBJECTS) $(LIB) -o command

main.o: command.h main.c

sub.o: command.h sub.c

lex.yy.o: command.h lex.yy.c

lex.yy.c: command.l
      lex command.l
```

```
y.tab.o: command.h y.tab.c

y.tab.c: command.y
      yacc command.y

clean:
      rm *.o

install:
      cp command $(BIN)
```

Index

15-09 i 2i -237-50